Volume equivalents

METRIC	IMPERIAL	METRIC	IMPERIAL
30ml	1fl oz	450ml	15fl oz
60ml	2fl oz	500ml	16fl oz
75ml	2½fl oz	600ml	1 pint
100ml	3½fl oz	750ml	1¼ pints
120ml	4fl oz	900ml	1½ pints
150ml	5fl oz (¼ pint)	1 litre	1¾ pints
175ml	6fl oz	1.2 litres	2 pints
200ml	7fl oz (⅓ pint)	1.4 litres	2½ pints
250ml	8fl oz	1.5 litres	2¾ pints
300ml	10fl oz (½ pint)	1.7 litres	3 pints
350ml	12fl oz	2 litres	3½ pints
400ml	14fl oz	3 litres	5¼ pints

Weight equivalents

METRIC	IMPERIAL	METRIC	IMPERIAL
15g	½oz	150g	5½oz
20g	¾oz	175g	6oz
25g	scant 1oz	200g	7oz
30g	1oz	225g	8oz
45g	1½oz	250g	9oz
50g	1⅓oz	300g	10oz
60g	2oz	450g	1lb
75g	2½oz	500g	1lb 2oz
85g	3oz	675g	1½lb
100g	3½oz	900g	2lb
115g	4oz	1kg	2¼lb
125g	4½oz	1.5kg	3lb 3oz
140g	5oz	1.8kg	4lb

To Sam,

You may need this one
day!

Happy 18th

The Kolnahans
XX 2011

everyday
easy
One-pot

everyday easy
One-pot

hearty soups • quick stir-fries • simple casseroles

LONDON, NEW YORK, MELBOURNE,
MUNICH, AND DELHI

Editor
Andrew Roff

Designer
Kathryn Wilding

Senior Jacket Creative
Nicola Powling

Managing Editor
Dawn Henderson

Managing Art Editor
Christine Keilty

Production Editor
Ben Marcus

Production Controller
Hema Gohil

Creative Technical Support
Sonia Charbonnier

DK INDIA

Head of Publishing
Aparna Sharma

Design Manager
Romi Chakraborty

Designer
Neha Ahuja

DTP Co-ordinator
Balwant Singh

DTP Designer
Tarun Sharma

Material first published in *The Cooking Book* in 2008
This edition first published in Great Britain in 2009
by Dorling Kindersley Limited
80 Strand, London WC2R 0RL

A Penguin Company
Copyright © 2008, 2009 Dorling Kindersley
Text copyright © 2008, 2009 Dorling Kindersley

2 4 6 8 10 9 7 5 3

A CIP catalogue record for this book
is available from the British Library.

ISBN 978-1-4053-4526-2

Colour reproduction by MDP, Bath
Printed and bound in Singapore by Star Standard

Discover more at
www.dk.com

CONTENTS

Soups, stews, casseroles, stir-fries – all delicious and all require just one pot to make. Cooking all the ingredients in a pot allows their flavours to mingle, infuse, and develop, making one-pot meals some of the tastiest. A one-pot recipe may involve maybe another pan or bowl to brown meat, fry onions, or whip eggs but all the components finally meet in one pot to produce something good. Bring the pot to the kitchen table, lift the lid, and tuck in.

As well as the superb taste, one-pot meals have many practical benefits – get on with something else while your pot bubbles away in the oven or on the hob, enjoy your meal without the thought of the washing up waiting for you (with just one pot, there won't be much!), and easily divide the contents of the pot into as many dishes as people you need to feed, or save any leftovers for tomorrow's lunch.

The popularity of one-pot cooking is far and wide. Some of the world's best-loved dishes involve slow-cooking in one pot – Chilli Con Carne, Irish Stew, and Osso Bucco are prime examples. Other one-pot recipes seem exotic and adventurous but are just as simple to make – Kedgeree and Pad Thai require the bear minimum of equipment and hardly any cooking. Whatever you fancy, the recipes on the following pages won't disappoint.

The book begins with a selection of step-by-step **Techniques** that will refine your core cookery skills. Properly done, these techniques will cut your preparation time in half and ensure you get the most from your ingredients. Some techniques are simple, those kitchen tasks involved in many recipes, such as peeling and chopping garlic and dicing an onion. Other techniques are more specialized, revealing the secrets to perfect pasta, stir-fried vegetables, and fresh tomato sauce.

A selection of **Recipe Choosers** follows – galleries that showcase recipes so you can quickly find something that takes your fancy. Organized according to key ingredient, these are perfect if you find yourself with a particular inkling for fish, pasta, meat, pulses, or chicken, for example.

The first recipes use storecupbaord ingredients or everyday items that you would pick up on your weekly shop. This **Budget** section will produce impressive, nutritious family food without great expense. Macaroni Cheese and Tuna and Pasta Bake are particular family favourites that cost very little to make.

Next comes the **Hearty** section. Beans and other pulses can be loaded with a variety of flavours and make for hearty food that is perfect for satisfying hunger pangs. Serve these meals, such as Tuscan Bean Soup and Vegetable Biryani, in bowls and leave plenty in the pot to keep warm so the family can return for seconds (and probably thirds) when they want to – great for cold winter evenings.

After a busy day, turn to the **Super Quick** section where you'll find a collection of recipes you can convert from ingredients to meal in minutes. Singapore Noodles and Thai Green Chicken Curry are favourite recipes that you can rustle up in moments.

Choose something low in fat or GI from the **Healthy** section, packed with tantalizing recipes that you can proudly feed to your family. With such delights as Spaghetti Mare e Monti and Swordfish Baked with Herbs, these recipes are as irresistible as they are nutritious.

Lastly, you'll find a selection of recipes that will go down a treat when entertaining. Bouillabaisse and Moules Marinières are simple to prepare and guarantee to **Impress**. And what could be better for you, the host, when entertaining than a one-pot recipe? Enjoy a glass of wine with your friends as your meal cooks away in the kitchen. Many one-pot meals won't spoil from a few extra minutes cooking so you can serve your food when you're ready for it.

One-pot meals are designed to be shared. Put the pot on the kitchen table and let the family help themselves – a dinnertime ritual to bring everyone together to enjoy great food.

A guide to symbols

The recipes in this book are accompanied by symbols that alert you to important information.

 Tells you how many people the recipe serves, or how much is produced.

 Indicates how much time you will need to prepare and cook a dish. Next to this symbol you will also find out if additional time is required for such things as marinating, standing, or cooling. You will have to read the recipe to find out exactly how much extra time is needed.

 Points out nutritional benefits, such as low fat or low GI.

 This is especially important, as it alerts you to what has to be done before you can begin to cook the recipe. For example, you may need to soak some beans overnight.

 This denotes that special equipment is required, such as a deep-fat fryer or skewers. Where possible, alternatives are given.

 This symbol accompanies freezing information.

Oven temperature equivalents

CELSIUS	FAHRENHEIT	GAS	DESCRIPTION
110°C	225°F	$\frac{1}{4}$	Cool
130°C	250°F	$\frac{1}{2}$	Cool
140°C	275°F	1	Very low
150°C	300°F	2	Very low
160°C	325°F	3	Low
180°C	350°F	4	Moderate
190°C	375°F	5	Moderately hot
200°C	400°F	6	Hot
220°C	425°F	7	Hot
230°C	450°F	8	Very hot
240°C	475°F	9	Very hot

Refrigerator and freezer storage guide

FOOD	REFRIGERATOR	FREEZER
Raw poultry, fish, and meat (small pieces)	2–3 days	3–6 months
Raw minced beef and poultry	1–2 days	3 months
Cooked whole roasts or whole poultry	2–3 days	9 months
Cooked poultry pieces	1–2 days	1 month (6 months in stock or gravy)
Soups and stews	2–3 days	1–3 months
Casseroles	2–3 days	2–4 weeks

Volume equivalents

METRIC	IMPERIAL	METRIC	IMPERIAL
30ml	1fl oz	300ml	10fl oz ($^1/_2$ pint)
60ml	2fl oz	350ml	12fl oz
75ml	$2^1/_2$fl oz	400ml	14fl oz
100ml	$3^1/_2$fl oz	450ml	15fl oz
120ml	4fl oz	500ml	16fl oz
150ml	5fl oz ($^1/_4$ pint)	600ml	1 pint
175ml	6fl oz	750ml	$1^1/_4$ pints
200ml	7fl oz ($^1/_3$ pint)	900ml	$1^1/_2$ pints
250ml	8fl oz	1 litre	$1^3/_4$ pints

Weight equivalents

METRIC	IMPERIAL	METRIC	IMPERIAL
25g	scant 1oz	125g	$4^1/_2$oz
30g	1oz	140g	5oz
45g	$1^1/_2$oz	150g	$5^1/_2$oz
50g	$1^1/_3$oz	175g	6oz
60g	2oz	200g	7oz
75g	$2^1/_2$oz	225g	8oz
85g	3oz	250g	9oz
100g	$3^1/_2$oz	450g	1lb
115g	4oz	1kg	$2^1/_4$lb

TECHNIQUES

Peel and chop garlic

Garlic is essential to many recipes and peeling and chopping it is easy once you know how. The finer you chop garlic, the more flavour you'll release.

1 Place each clove flat on a cutting board. Place a large knife blade on top and pound it with the palm of your hand. Discard the skin and cut off the ends.

2 Slice the clove into slivers lengthways, then cut across into tiny chunks. Collect the pieces into a pile and chop again for finer pieces.

Dice an onion

Once an onion is halved, it can be sliced or diced. This technique is for quick dicing, which helps prevent your eyes watering.

1 Using a sharp chef's knife, cut the onion lengthways in half and peel. Lay one half cut-side down. Make a few slices horizontally, cutting up to the root, then slice down vertically, cutting up to the root.

2 Cut across the vertical slices to produce an even dice. Use the root to hold the onion steady, then discard when all the onion is diced.

Deseed and cut chillies

Chillies contain capsaicin, which gives off a fiery heat. Always wash your hands immediately after handling chillies.

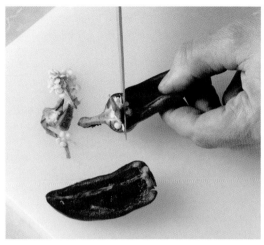

1 Cut the chilli lengthways in half. Using the tip of your knife, scrape out the seeds and remove the membrane and stem.

2 Flatten each chilli half with the palm of your hand and slice lengthways into strips. For dice, hold the strips together and slice crossways.

Prepare bell peppers

Red, green, orange, and yellow peppers add brilliant colour and sweetness to stir-fries, and distinctive flavour to many dishes.

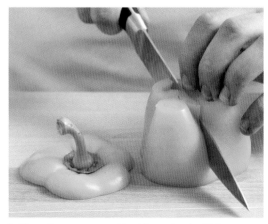

1 Place the pepper on its side and cut off the top and bottom. Stand the pepper on one of the cut ends and slice it in half lengthways. Remove the core and seeds.

2 Open each section and lay them flat on the cutting board. Remove the remaining pale, fleshy ribs. Cut the peppers into smaller sections, following the divisions of the pepper.

13

Peel and deseed tomatoes

Before using tomatoes for sauces or soups they must be peeled and deseeded. Prepare your tomatoes by removing the stem, then score an "X" at their base.

1 Immerse the tomato in a pan of boiling water for 20 seconds. With a slotted spoon, remove the tomato and place it into a bowl of iced water.

2 When cool enough to handle, use a paring knife to peel away the loosened skin. Cut each tomato in half and gently squeeze out the seeds.

Make fresh tomato sauce

The combination of tomatoes and a few other ingredients makes a great sauce. This recipe makes 600ml (1 pint). Once cooked, heat thoroughly before serving.

In a saucepan over low heat, place 25g (scant 1oz) unsalted butter, 2 chopped shallots, 1 tbsp olive oil, 1 bay leaf, and 3 crushed garlic cloves. Stir, cover, and sweat for 5–6 minutes. Add 1kg (2¼ lb) chopped and deseeded ripe plum tomatoes to the pan with 2 tbsp tomato purée and 1 tbsp sugar. Cook for 5 minutes, stirring, then add 250ml (8fl oz) water and bring to the boil. Reduce the heat and simmer for 30 minutes, then season to taste with salt and pepper. Using a ladle, press the sauce through a sieve and serve.

Chop herbs

Chop fresh herbs just before using to release their flavour and aroma. You may wish to reserve a small amount to use as a garnish for the finished dish.

1 Strip the leaves from the stems and gather them together in a tight pile. Roll the pile into a cigar-shaped bundle.

2 Using a large sharp knife, chop through the herbs using a rocking motion. Gather and repeat to achieve the desired size.

Stir-fry vegetables

This low-fat cooking method uses very little oil so the vegetables retain their natural flavours and take hardly any time to cook.

1 When the wok (or pan) is hot, add a little sunflower, rapeseed, or groundnut oil, tilting the pan to coat the base. When very hot, toss in garlic, ginger, chilli, or spring onions.

2 Add the desired vegetables and use a spatula to toss continually. When stir-frying green vegetables, such as broccoli, add a couple of tbsp of water and cover. Cook until just tender and still crisp.

Chicken stock

By simmering the remains of your roast with a few vegetables and herbs, you can produce a stock from scratch for soups and risottos.

1 Add either raw chicken bones, the carcass, or the bones and scraps from a cooked chicken into a large stockpot with carrots, celery, onions, and a bouquet garni of fresh herbs. Add water and bring to the boil.

2 Simmer for 2–3 hours, skimming frequently. Ladle through a fine sieve and season to taste. Let cool and refrigerate for up to 3 days. Lift any congealed fat from the surface with a slotted spoon.

Vegetable stock

Simmering water with vegetables will capture their delicate flavour. Use the stock to flavour soups and risottos when preparing vegetarian meals.

1 Place chopped carrots, celery, onion, and a bouquet garni into a large stockpot. Cover with water and bring to the boil. Reduce the heat and simmer the stock for up to 1 hour.

2 Ladle through a fine sieve, pressing the vegetables against the sieve to extract any extra liquid. Season to taste with salt and freshly ground black pepper, let cool, and refrigerate for up to 3 days.

Fish stock

Keep the parts of your fish you don't use in cooking to make a stock – perfect for using in seafood soups and stews.

1 Cut the fish bones and trimmings into equal-sized pieces. Place them in a bowl of cold, salted water to absorb moisture and remove any blood. Drain and place the bones and trimmings into a large stockpot.

2 Cut carrots, celery, and onion into pieces of equal size and add them (and any other flavourings you wish) into the pan with the fish. Cover with water, turn up the heat, and bring to the boil.

3 Once the stock reaches the boil, lower the heat and simmer for 20 minutes (any longer and the stock will start to become bitter). Skim off the scum that rises to the surface with a slotted spoon.

4 Ladle through a fine sieve, pressing the solids against the sieve to extract any extra liquid. Season to taste with salt and freshly ground black pepper, let cool, and refrigerate for up to 3 days.

Soak and cook rice

To cook perfect rice, use $1\frac{1}{2}$ times as much water or stock as rice. Always be sure to soak and rinse the rice before cooking.

Put the rice and liquid into a large saucepan. Over moderate heat, bring to the boil, stir once, and lower the heat to simmer uncovered for 10–12 minutes, or until all the liquid is absorbed. Remove from the heat and cover with a clean, folded tea towel and a fitted lid. Leave the rice to steam, without removing the lid, for 20 minutes. Remove the folded tea towel and replace the lid. Leave the rice to sit for 5 minutes, covered. Fluff the rice with a fork and serve.

Boil noodles

Noodles need to be soaked in hot water or boiled for a few minutes before using. Rinsing under cold water refreshes them.

1 To boil egg, wheat, or buckwheat noodles, bring a large saucepan of water to the boil. Add the noodles, return to the boil, then cook until the noodles are softened and flexible, about 2 minutes.

2 Drain the noodles in a colander and place them under cold, running water. Toss the noodles with a little oil to prevent them from sticking, then serve or proceed with the recipe.

Cook dried pasta

Dried pasta is essential to have in your storecupboard, as it can form the basis of many quick dishes, but it's all too easy to overcook it.

1 Bring a large pan of salted water to the boil and gently pour in the pasta. Boil uncovered, following the recommended cook time on the packet, or until *al dente* when tasted.

2 As soon as the pasta is *al dente*, quickly drain it through a colander, shaking gently to remove any excess water. Toss the pasta with a little oil, then serve or proceed with the recipe.

Make couscous

With no cooking on the hob or in the oven, couscous has to be the easiest and fastest side dish. Use around 1³/₄ times as much water as couscous.

1 Pour the quick-cook couscous and a pinch of salt into a large bowl and pour over boiling water. Cover with a folded tea towel, leave for 5 minutes, remove the tea towel, and fluff up with a fork.

2 Re-cover the bowl and leave for another 5 minutes. Remove the tea towel and add either 1 tbsp olive oil or a knob of unsalted butter and fluff up the couscous again until light. Serve.

Pasta and noodles

Spaghetti mare e monti
page 160

Tuna and pasta bake page 44

Pappardelle ragù page 68

Stracciatella with pasta page 120

Pad Thai page 72

Macaroni bake with ham and peppers page 70

Mediterranean lasagne page 184

Thai noodle stir-fry page 48

Singapore noodles page 124

Spaghetti puttanesca page 50

Fideua page 164

Pasta alla carbonara page 122

Pulses, rice, and grains

Puy lentils with goat's cheese, olives, and fresh thyme page 128

Quinoa tabbouleh page 126

Minestrone page 40

Hoppin' John page 96

Vegetable biryani page 78

Lentil salad with lemon and almonds page 156

Kasha with vegetables page 158

Kedgeree page 76

Arroz con pollo page 172

Chicken and chickpea pilaf page 168

Paella page 188

Vegetarian

Mushroom soup page 34

Tofu and mushroom strogonoff page 46

Curried parsnip soup page 36

Porcini mushroom soup page 60

Macaroni cheese page 54

Vegetable curry page 74

Vegetable biryani page 78

Watercress soup page 118

Quinoa tabbouleh page 126

Puy lentils with goat's cheese, olives, and fresh thyme page 128

Tomato soup page 150

Kasha with vegetables page 158

Lentil soup page 154

Lentil salad with lemon and almonds page 156

Carrot and orange soup page 152

Chilli tofu stir-fry page 162

Winter vegetable soup page 42

Mediterranean lasagne page 184

Fish and shellfish

Swordfish baked with herbs
page 166

New England clam chowder
page 64

Sweet and sour prawns page 80

Shrimp diabolo page 82

Paella page 188

Cod in tomato sauce page 86

**Smoked haddock with spinach
and pancetta** page 132

Seafood curry page 134

Fisherman's tuna stew page 182

Baked bream page 200

Seafood and tomato stew page 84

Moules marinières page 190

Mussels with tomatoes and chilli page 198

Salt cod braised with vegetables page 196

Bouillabaisse page 180

27

Poultry and game

Chicken gumbo page 204

Chicken paprikash page 88

Thai green chicken curry
page 136

**Pot-roast guinea fowl with
cabbage and walnuts** page 94

Arroz con pollo page 172

Singapore noodles page 124

Grilled quail with ginger glaze page 206

Chicken casserole with herb dumplings page 92

Creamy tarragon chicken page 90

Chicken and chickpea pilaf page 168

Meat

Pork and leek pie page 52

Hoppin' John page 96

Braised lamb page 104

Roast lamb with flageolets page 100

Lamb tagine with couscous page 102

Navarin of lamb page 106

Meat loaf page 114

Thai red beef curry page 110

Irish stew page 108

Quick lamb curry page 140

Chinese chilli beef stir-fry page 142

Daube of beef with wild mushrooms page 210

Veal scaloppine page 212

Beef strogonoff page 208

Choucroute garni page 214

Osso bucco page 216

Mushroom soup

Using a selection of both wild and cultivated mushrooms will produce a soup that is bursting with flavour.

INGREDIENTS

30g (1oz) butter
1 onion, finely chopped
2 celery sticks, finely chopped
1 garlic clove, crushed
450g (1lb) mixed mushrooms,
  roughly chopped
200g (7oz) potatoes, peeled and cubed
1 litre (1¾ pints) vegetable stock
2 tbsp finely chopped parsley
salt and freshly ground black pepper

METHOD

1 Melt the butter in a large saucepan, add the onion, celery, and garlic, and fry for 3–4 minutes, or until softened.

2 Stir in the mushrooms and continue to fry for a further 5–6 minutes. Add the potatoes and stock and bring up to the boil. Reduce the heat and leave to simmer gently for 30 minutes.

3 Turn the heat off and allow the soup to cool slightly. Pour the soup into a blender of food processor and purée until smooth.

4 Sprinkle in the parsley and season to taste with salt and pepper. Serve immediately.

GOOD WITH Warm crusty rolls and a little horseradish cream in each bowl for added flavour and spice.

PREPARE AHEAD The soup can be kept covered in the refrigerator for 2–3 days and reheated to serve.

serves 4

prep 10 mins
• cook 45 mins

freeze for up to
3 months

34

Curried parsnip soup

The mix of sweet parsnips and gentle spices makes this soup a great winter warmer.

INGREDIENTS

1 onion
300g (10oz) parsnips
1 carrot
1 potato
45g (1½oz) butter
2 tbsp plain flour
2 tbsp mild curry powder
1.2 litres (2 pints) vegetable stock
crème fraîche, to serve
parsley, chopped, to serve

METHOD

1 Peel and roughly chop all the vegetables, keeping the onion separate.

2 Melt the butter in a large saucepan over a medium heat; add the onions, and cook, stirring frequently, until they are soft but not browned. Add the other vegetables, followed by the flour and curry powder and cook, stirring, for a further 2 minutes.

3 Gradually add the stock or water, stirring until well blended. Increase the heat and bring to the boil, then reduce the heat to a low simmer. Cover and leave to cook for 40 minutes, or until the vegetables are tender.

4 Turn the heat off, uncover, and allow the soup to cool slightly. Pour the soup into a blender or food processor and purée until completely smooth.

5 Reheat before serving, then pour into individual bowls. Add a swirl of crème fraîche and a scattering of chopped parsley.

GOOD WITH Crusty bread or cheese scones.

serves 4

prep 10 mins
• cook 50 mins

French onion soup

This Parisian classic is given extra punch with a spoonful of brandy in each bowl.

INGREDIENTS

30g (1oz) butter
1 tbsp sunflower oil
675g (1½lb) onions, thinly sliced
1 tsp sugar
salt and freshly ground black pepper
120ml (4fl oz) dry red wine
2 tbsp plain white flour
1.5 litres (2¾ pints) beef stock
4 tbsp brandy
1 garlic clove, cut in half
4 slices of baguette, about
    2cm (¾in) thick, toasted
115g (4oz) Gruyère cheese
    or Emmental cheese, grated

METHOD

1 Melt the butter with the oil in a large, heavy pan over a low heat. Stir together the onions and sugar and season to taste with salt and pepper. Press a piece of wet, greaseproof paper over the surface and cook, stirring occasionally, uncovered, for 40 minutes, or until the onions are rich and dark golden brown. Take care that they do not stick and burn on the bottom.

2 Remove the paper and stir in the wine. Increase the heat to medium and stir for 5 minutes, or until the onions are glazed. Sprinkle with the flour and stir for 2 minutes. Stir in the stock and bring to the boil. Reduce the heat to low, cover, and leave the soup to simmer for 30 minutes. Taste and adjust the seasoning, if necessary.

3 Meanwhile, preheat the grill on its highest setting. Divide the soup between the bowls and stir 1 tbsp brandy into each. Rub the garlic clove over the toast and place 1 slice in each bowl. Sprinkle with the cheese and grill for 2–3 minutes, or until the cheese is bubbling and golden. Serve at once.

PREPARE AHEAD Steps 1 and 2 can be completed up to 1 day in advance, covered and chilled.

serves 4

prep 10 mins
• cook 1 hr

4 flameproof
soup bowls

freeze the soup,
without the
bread or
cheese, for up
to 1 month

Minestrone

This substantial soup makes a great lunch or supper dish, and you can add whatever vegetables are in season.

INGREDIENTS

100g (3½oz) dried white cannellini beans
2 tbsp olive oil
2 celery sticks, finely chopped
2 carrots, finely chopped
1 onion, finely chopped
400g can chopped tomatoes
750ml (1¼ pints) chicken stock
   or vegetable stock
salt and freshly ground black pepper
60g (2oz) small short-cut pasta
4 tbsp chopped flat-leaf parsley
45g (1½oz) Parmesan cheese,
   finely grated

METHOD

1 Put the cannellini beans in a large bowl, cover with cold water, and leave to soak for at least 6 hours or overnight.

2 Drain the beans, place in a large saucepan, cover with cold water, and bring to the boil over a high heat, skimming the surface as necessary. Boil for 10 minutes, then reduce the heat to low, partially cover the pan, and leave the beans to simmer for 1 hour, or until just tender. Drain well and set aside.

3 Heat the oil in the rinsed-out pan over a medium heat. Add the celery, carrots, and onion and fry, stirring occasionally, for 5 minutes, or until tender. Stir in the beans, the tomatoes with their juice, the stock, and season to taste with salt and pepper. Bring to the boil, stirring, then cover and leave to simmer for 20 minutes.

4 Add the pasta and simmer for a further 10–15 minutes, or until cooked but still tender to the bite. Stir in the parsley and half the Parmesan, then adjust the seasoning. Serve hot, sprinkled with the remaining Parmesan.

PREPARE AHEAD Steps 1 and 2 can be done 1 day before.

serves 4–6

prep 20 mins,
plus soaking
• cook 1¾ hrs

soak the beans
before starting
the recipe

freeze for up to
1 month before
the pasta is
added in step 4

Winter vegetable soup

Some people call this "Penny Soup", not just because it is inexpensive to make but because the vegetables resemble coins.

INGREDIENTS

1 leek
300g (10oz) new potatoes
250g (9oz) large carrots
175g (6oz) small sweet potatoes
15g (1/2oz) butter
1 tbsp olive oil
600ml (1 pint) vegetable stock
1 tbsp chopped parsley
salt and freshly ground black pepper

METHOD

1 Slice all the vegetables across into rounds about 2–3mm (1/8in) thick. The potatoes can be left peeled or unpeeled.

2 Melt the butter with the oil in a large saucepan or flameproof casserole and add the leeks. Cook over a medium heat for 3–4 minutes, or until soft, stirring frequently. Add the remaining vegetables and cook, stirring, for 1 minute.

3 Pour in the stock, bring to the boil, cover, and simmer for 18–20 minutes, or until the vegetables are tender but not soft.

4 Transfer about one-third of the vegetables into a blender or food processor with a little of the liquid. Blend to a smooth purée and return to the pan. Stir in the parsley, season to taste with salt and pepper, and serve, with the vegetables in a little mound in the centre.

PREPARE AHEAD Cook the day before, cool, cover, and refrigerate. Reheat before serving.

serves 4

prep 15 mins
• cook 25 mins

Tuna and pasta bake

This is a quick, one-dish storecupboard meal that is ideal
at the end of a busy day.

INGREDIENTS

200g (7oz) pasta shells
300g can condensed cream
  of mushroom soup
120ml (4fl oz) milk
200g can tuna in brine, drained and flaked
200g can sweetcorn, drained and rinsed
1 onion, finely chopped
1 red pepper, cored and finely chopped
4 tbsp chopped flat-leaf parsley
pinch of chilli powder (optional)
115g (4oz) Cheddar cheese
  or Cheshire cheese, grated
salt and freshly ground black pepper

METHOD

1 Bring a large saucepan of salted water to the boil over a high heat. Add the pasta, stir,
and cook for 2 minutes less than the time specified on the packet.

2 Meanwhile, preheat the oven to 220°C (425°F/Gas 7) and grease a 1.5 litre (2³/₄ pint)
ovenproof serving dish.

3 Drain the pasta and set it aside. Heat the mushroom soup and milk over a low heat in the
same saucepan. Add the tuna, sweetcorn, onion, pepper, parsley, chilli powder, if using, and half
of the cheese, and stir. Once the soup is heated, stir in the cooked pasta. Season to taste with salt
and pepper.

4 Tip the mixture into the prepared dish and smooth the top. Sprinkle with the remaining cheese.
Place the dish in the oven and bake for 30–35 minutes, or until the top is golden brown. Serve hot,
straight from the dish.

GOOD WITH Hot garlic bread and a tossed green salad on the side.

PREPARE AHEAD The whole dish can be assembled, covered, and chilled several hours
in advance. Remove the dish from the refrigerator at least 10 minutes before cooking.

serves 6

prep 10 mins
• cook 40 mins

Tofu and mushroom strogonoff

This recipe gives the traditional strogonoff a tasty vegetarian twist by substituting tofu chunks for the meat.

INGREDIENTS

2 tbsp sunflower oil
350g (12oz) firm tofu, cut into
    strips or bite-sized cubes
1 red onion, thinly sliced
2 garlic cloves, crushed
1 red pepper, deseeded and sliced
1 orange pepper, deseeded and sliced
250g (9oz) mixed mushrooms, quartered
2 tbsp tomato purée
2 tbsp smooth peanut butter
150ml (5fl oz) vegetable stock
2 tsp cornflour
200g (7oz) crème fraîche
    or Greek-style natural yogurt
salt and freshly ground black pepper
chives, to serve
200g (7oz) long-grain rice, boiled to serve

METHOD

1 Heat 1 tbsp of the oil in a large frying pan or wok and stir-fry the tofu over a fairly brisk heat until golden. Remove from the pan and set aside.

2 Add the rest of the oil to the pan, reduce the heat, and add the onion and garlic. Fry until softened, add the peppers and mushrooms, and fry for 5 minutes, stirring frequently.

3 Add the tomato purée and peanut butter and return the tofu to the pan. Stir in the stock.

4 Mix the cornflour to a paste with a little water and stir in to the pan. Simmer for 2–3 minutes.

5 Stir in the crème fraîche or yogurt, season to taste with salt and pepper, and simmer for 2 minutes. Sprinkle with chives and serve with rice.

serves 4

prep 15 mins
• cook 20 mins

Thai noodle stir-fry

A fragrant and colourful stir-fry with the flavours of Thailand.

INGREDIENTS

175g (6oz) thin rice noodles
1 stalk lemongrass
3 tbsp groundnut oil or vegetable oil
3 skinless boneless chicken breasts,
    cut into thin strips
1 onion, sliced
1 tsp finely grated root ginger
1 fresh red chilli, deseeded and finely chopped
1 orange pepper, deseeded and sliced
115g (4oz) shiitake mushrooms, sliced
2 heads of pak choi, shredded
2 tbsp light soy sauce
1 tbsp Thai fish sauce
1 tsp sweet chilli sauce

METHOD

1 Soak the noodles in a bowl of boiling water until softened, or as directed on the packet. Drain and set aside. Meanwhile, remove and discard the outer leaves of the lemongrass and trim away the tough woody end. Finely chop.

2 Heat 2 tbsp of the oil in a wok and stir-fry the chicken over a high heat for 2–3 minutes, or until lightly browned. Remove from the pan and set aside.

3 Reduce the heat to medium, add the remaining oil, and stir-fry the onion for 2 minutes. Add the lemongrass, ginger, chilli, orange pepper, and mushrooms, and stir-fry for 2 minutes.

4 Add the pak choi and stir-fry for a further 2 minutes, then return the chicken to the pan and add the noodles. Pour in the soy sauce, fish sauce, and sweet chilli sauce, and toss everything together over the heat for 2–3 minutes, or until piping hot and the chicken is cooked through. Serve at once.

serves 4

prep 20 mins
• cook 15 mins

low fat

Spaghetti puttanesca

This spicy pasta dish is popular in Italy.

INGREDIENTS

4 tbsp extra virgin olive oil
2 garlic cloves, finely chopped
$\frac{1}{2}$ fresh red chilli, deseeded
   and finely chopped
6 canned anchovies, drained
   and finely chopped
115g (4oz) black olives,
   pitted and chopped
1–2 tbsp capers, rinsed and drained
450g (1lb) tomatoes, skinned,
   deseeded, and chopped
450g (1lb) spaghetti
chopped parsley, to serve
Parmesan cheese, to serve

METHOD

1 Heat the oil in a saucepan, add the garlic and chilli, and cook gently for 2 minutes, or until the garlic is slightly coloured. Add all the other sauce ingredients and stir, breaking down the anchovies to a paste.

2 Reduce the heat and let the sauce simmer, uncovered, for 10–15 minutes, or until the sauce has thickened, stirring frequently.

3 Cook the spaghetti in plenty of lightly salted boiling water for 10 minutes, or as directed on the packet. Drain.

4 Toss the spaghetti with the sauce, and serve sprinkled with parsley and Parmesan cheese.

GOOD WITH A simple spinach salad and crusty bread.

serves 4

prep 15 mins
• cook 25 mins

Pork and leek pie

This classic chunky pie has a crisp crust and a wholesome flavour.

INGREDIENTS

2 tbsp vegetable oil
450g (1lb) lean boneless pork steaks,
  cut into 2.5cm (1in) cubes
2 leeks, thickly sliced
150g (5$\frac{1}{2}$oz) mushrooms, halved
1 tsp thyme leaves
150ml (5fl oz) chicken stock
1 tbsp cornflour, mixed with 1 tbsp water
250ml (8fl oz) apple juice
2 tbsp tomato purée
salt and freshly ground black pepper
250g (9oz) ready-made shortcrust pastry
1 egg, beaten, to glaze

METHOD

1 Heat the oil in a frying pan. Brown the pork, remove, and set aside. Add the vegetables and thyme, and fry for 5 minutes. Add the stock, cornflour, juice, and tomato purée, and bring to the boil, stirring until thickened. Return the pork, season with salt and pepper, and simmer for 25 minutes.

2 Transfer the pork and vegetables to a pie dish, reserving the sauce. Roll out the pastry and use to cover the dish, decorating the top with the trimmings. Make a steam hole in the pastry, glaze with the egg, and chill for 30 minutes. Preheat the oven to 200°C (400°F/Gas 6). Bake for 35 minutes, or until the pastry is golden, and serve with the sauce.

GOOD WITH Steamed vegetables, such as broccoli and carrots.

serves 4

prep 25 mins,
plus cooling
• cook 1 hr
10 mins

Macaroni cheese

This simple dish makes a nourishing family meal.

INGREDIENTS

400g (14oz) dried macaroni
85g (3oz) butter
100g (3½oz) fresh breadcrumbs
4 tbsp plain flour
1 tsp mustard powder
pinch of ground nutmeg
400ml (14fl oz) milk, warmed
175g (6oz) Cheddar cheese, coarsely grated
100g (3½oz) mozzarella cheese, drained and finely diced
60g (2oz) Parmesan cheese, coarsely grated

METHOD

1 Bring a large pan of lightly salted water to the boil over a high heat. Add the macaroni and boil for 2 minutes less than specified on the packet. Drain well and set aside, shaking off any excess water.

2 Meanwhile, preheat the oven to 200°C (400°F/Gas 6) and grease an ovenproof serving dish. Melt 25g (scant 1oz) of the butter in a small pan. Add the breadcrumbs, stir, then remove the pan from the heat and set aside.

3 Melt the remaining butter in a large saucepan over a medium heat. Sprinkle over the flour, then stir for 30 seconds. Stir in the mustard powder and nutmeg, then remove the pan from the heat and slowly whisk in the milk. Return the pan to the heat and bring the mixture to the boil, whisking, for 2–3 minutes, or until the sauce thickens. Remove from the heat. Stir in the Cheddar cheese, until melted and smooth, then add the macaroni and mozzarella and stir together.

4 Transfer the mixture to the prepared dish and smooth the surface. Toss the breadcrumbs with the Parmesan cheese and sprinkle over the top. Place the dish on a baking sheet and bake for 25 minutes, or until heated through and golden brown on top. Leave to stand for 2 minutes, then serve straight from the dish.

GOOD WITH A green salad or garlic bread.

PREPARE AHEAD The whole dish can be assembled up to a day in advance and refrigerated for last-minute cooking. Add the fresh breadcrumbs and cheese topping just before baking.

serves 6

prep 20 mins
• cook 35 mins

Herb and goat's cheese frittata

Thinner than a Spanish tortilla, this popular Italian dish is ideal for lunch or a light supper.

INGREDIENTS

6 eggs
4 sage leaves, finely chopped
salt and freshly ground black pepper
3 tbsp olive oil, plus extra for brushing
1 shallot, chopped
10 cherry tomatoes, halved
115g (4oz) goat's cheese, rind removed
   if necessary, and crumbled

METHOD

1 Preheat the grill on its highest setting and position the rack 10cm (4in) from the heat. Beat the eggs in a bowl with the sage, season to taste with salt and pepper, and set aside.

2 Heat the oil in the frying pan over a medium heat. Add the shallot and fry, stirring constantly, for 3 minutes, or until just softened but not browned.

3 Add the eggs to the pan and stir gently to combine. Reduce the heat, then cover and leave to cook gently for 10–15 minutes before removing the lid; the frittata should still be runny on top.

4 Arrange the tomatoes and goat's cheese over the surface and lightly brush with olive oil. Transfer the pan to the grill for 5 minutes or until the frittata is set and lightly browned. Leave to stand for 5 minutes before cutting into wedges. Serve warm or cooled.

GOOD WITH Plenty of Italian bread and a tomato salad.

serves 4

prep 10 mins
• cook 20 mins

23cm (9in)
non-stick frying
pan with a lid
and flameproof
handle

Porcini mushroom soup

This hearty Italian country soup is full of deep, earthy goodness.

INGREDIENTS

30g (1oz) dried porcini mushrooms
3 tbsp extra virgin olive oil, plus extra to finish
2 onions, finely chopped
2 tsp chopped rosemary leaves
1 tsp thyme leaves
2 garlic cloves, finely sliced
115g (4oz) chestnut mushrooms, sliced
2 celery sticks with leaves, finely chopped
400g (14oz) can chopped tomatoes
750ml (1¼ pints) vegetable stock
salt and freshly ground black pepper
½ stale ciabatta or small crusty white loaf,
    torn into chunks

METHOD

1 Put the dried porcini in a heatproof bowl, pour over 300ml (10fl oz) boiling water, and leave to stand for 30 minutes. Drain, reserving the soaking liquid, then chop any large pieces of mushroom.

2 Heat the oil in a saucepan, add the onions, cover, and leave to cook for 10 minutes, or until soft. Add the rosemary, thyme, garlic, chestnut mushrooms, and celery, and continue cooking, uncovered, until the celery has softened.

3 Add the tomatoes, porcini, and stock. Strain the soaking liquid through muslin or a fine sieve into the pan. Bring to the boil, then lower the heat and simmer gently for 45 minutes.

4 Season to taste with salt and pepper, and add the bread. Remove the pan from the heat. Cover and leave to stand for 10 minutes before serving. Spoon into deep bowls and drizzle each serving with a little olive oil.

GOOD WITH Bowls of spiced olives and white crusty bread.

PREPARE AHEAD You can make the soup to the end of step 3 up to 2 days in advance; keep chilled until needed and reheat when ready to serve.

serves 4

prep 20 mins,
plus standing
• cook 1 hr

low fat, low GI

freeze, without
the bread, for
up to 3 months

Tuscan bean soup

This classic dish, *Ribollita*, is named after the traditional method of re-boiling soup from the day before.

INGREDIENTS

4 tbsp extra virgin olive oil,
    plus extra for drizzling
1 onion, chopped
2 carrots, sliced
1 leek, sliced
2 garlic cloves, chopped
400g can chopped tomatoes
1 tbsp tomato purée
900ml (1½ pints) chicken stock
salt and freshly ground black pepper
400g can borlotti beans, flageolet beans,
    or cannellini beans, drained and rinsed
250g (9oz) baby spinach leaves
    or spring greens, shredded
8 slices ciabatta bread
grated Parmesan cheese, for sprinkling

METHOD

1 Heat the oil in a large saucepan and fry the onion, carrot, and leek over a low heat for 10 minutes, or until softened but not coloured. Add the garlic and fry for 1 minute. Add the tomatoes, tomato purée, and stock. Season to taste with salt and pepper.

2 Mash half the beans with a fork and add to the pan. Bring to the boil, then lower the heat and simmer for 30 minutes.

3 Add the remaining beans and spinach to the pan. Simmer for a further 30 minutes.

4 Toast the bread until golden, place 2 pieces in each soup bowl, and drizzle with olive oil.

5 To serve, spoon the soup into the bowls, top with a sprinkling of Parmesan, and drizzle with a little more olive oil.

PREPARE AHEAD This soup improves with reheating, so it benefits from being made 1 day in advance. Reheat gently over a low heat.

serves 4

prep 15 mins
• cook 1 hr
20 mins

New England clam chowder

Americans often serve this traditional, creamy soup with small oyster-shaped saltine crackers.

INGREDIENTS
36 live clams
1 tbsp oil
115g (4oz) thick-cut rindless
   streaky bacon rashers, diced
1 onion, finely chopped
2 floury potatoes, such as King Edward,
   peeled and cut into 1cm (½in) cubes
2 tbsp plain white flour
600ml (1 pint) whole milk
salt and freshly ground black pepper
125ml (4½fl oz) single cream
2 tbsp finely chopped flat-leaf parsley

METHOD
1 Discard any open clams. Shuck the clams and reserve the juice, adding enough water to make 600ml (1 pint). Chop the clams.

2 Heat the oil in a large, heavy saucepan. Fry the bacon over a medium heat, stirring frequently, for 5 minutes, or until crisp. Remove the bacon from the pan with a slotted spoon, drain on kitchen paper and set aside.

3 Add the onion and potatoes to the pan and fry for 5 minutes, or until the onion has softened. Add the flour and stir for 2 minutes.

4 Stir in the clam juice and milk and season to taste with salt and pepper. Cover the pan, reduce the heat and leave to simmer for 20 minutes or until the potatoes are tender. Add the clams and simmer gently, uncovered, for 5 minutes.

5 Stir in the cream and heat through without boiling. Serve hot, sprinkled with bacon and parsley.

GOOD WITH Crumbled saltines or cream crackers.

serves 4

prep 15 mins
• cook 35 mins

cook clams on
day of purchase

Spanish stew

A filling one-pot meal known as *Cocido* in Spain.

INGREDIENTS

4 tbsp olive oil

4 small onions, quartered

2 garlic cloves, sliced

4 thick slices belly pork,
   about 500g (1lb 2oz) in total

4 chicken thighs, about 300g
   (10oz) in total

250g (9oz) beef braising steak,
   cut into 4 slices

175g (6oz) tocino or smoked streaky
   bacon, cut into 4 pieces

4 small pork spare ribs, 150g (5½oz) in total

100ml (3½fl oz) white wine

175g (6oz) chorizo,
   cut into 4 pieces

175g (6oz) morcilla
   (Spanish black pudding)

small ham bone

1 bay leaf

salt and freshly ground black pepper

8 small waxy potatoes

4 carrots, halved lengthways

400g can chickpeas, drained

1 Savoy cabbage or green
   cabbage heart, quartered

3 tbsp chopped parsley, to garnish

METHOD

1 Heat 1 tbsp oil in a large saucepan with the onions and garlic and fry for 10 minutes, stirring occasionally. Heat the remaining oil in a frying pan and fry the pork, chicken, beef, tocino, and spare ribs in batches until lightly browned on all sides, then transfer to the pan with the onions.

2 Add the wine into the frying pan, reduce by half, then pour into the saucepan. Add the chorizo, morcilla, ham bone, and bay leaf, season to taste with salt and pepper, then pour in enough cold water to cover. Bring to boil, then simmer, covered, for 1 hour 30 minutes. Add the potatoes and carrots to the pan, continue to cook for 30 minutes, then add the chickpeas and cabbage, and cook for 15 minutes.

3 To serve, remove the bay leaf and ham bone and divide the meat and vegetables between serving plates. Add a few spoonfuls of the hot broth and sprinkle with parsley.

GOOD WITH Yorkshire puddings, roast potatoes, and vegetables of your choice.

serves 6–8

prep 25 mins
• cook 2 hrs
45 mins

Pappardelle ragù

The rich, meaty, slow-simmered sauce goes well with spaghetti or tagliatelle, or used in a lasagne.

INGREDIENTS

30g (1oz) butter
2 tbsp olive oil
100g (3½oz) pancetta, diced
1 small onion, finely chopped
1 celery stick, finely chopped
1 carrot, finely chopped
2 garlic cloves, crushed
400g (14oz) lean beef steak, minced
100ml (3½fl oz) beef stock
2 tbsp tomato purée
400g can chopped tomatoes
salt and freshly ground black pepper
75ml (2½fl oz) milk, warmed
450g (1lb) dried pappardelle pasta
Parmesan cheese, grated, to serve

METHOD

1 Melt the butter with the oil in a deep, heavy saucepan and fry the pancetta for 1–2 minutes. Add the onion, celery, carrot, and garlic, and continue to fry, stirring occasionally, for 10 minutes, or until softened but not browned.

2 Stir in the meat, breaking up any lumps, then cook for a further 10 minutes, or until it is evenly coloured, stirring frequently. Stir in the stock, tomato purée, and tomatoes, season to taste with salt and pepper, then bring to the boil.

3 Reduce the heat to very low, cover the pan, and simmer very gently for 1½ hours. Stir occasionally to prevent sticking, adding more stock, if necessary. Stir the milk into the ragù, cover, and simmer for a further 30 minutes.

4 Bring a large pan of boiling, lightly salted water to the boil. Add the pappardelle and simmer for 8–10 minutes, or until cooked but still firm to the bite. Drain well, spoon the ragù over, and serve with freshly grated Parmesan.

serves 4

prep 15 mins
• cook 2 hrs

freeze the
sauce for up to
3 months

Macaroni bake with ham and peppers

Quick to make and full of rich flavours, this pasta bake makes a satisfying mid-week meal or an informal dinner party dish.

INGREDIENTS

400g (14oz) dried macaroni
salt and freshly ground black pepper
1 tbsp olive oil
1 red onion, thinly sliced
1 garlic clove, crushed
1 red pepper, thinly sliced
400g can chopped tomatoes
250g (9oz) piece smoked ham, diced
3 tbsp dry white wine or stock
2 tsp dried oregano
75g (2½oz) fresh white breadcrumbs
3 tbsp freshly grated Parmesan cheese
2 tbsp melted butter

METHOD

1 Preheat the oven to 200°C (400°F/Gas 6). Bring a large saucepan of lightly salted water to the boil, then add the macaroni. Simmer for 8–10 minutes, or according to packet instructions, until cooked but still firm to the bite. Drain well.

2 Meanwhile, heat the oil in a saucepan and fry the onion, garlic, and red pepper over a medium heat, stirring often, for 5 minutes, or until softened but not browned.

3 Add the tomatoes, ham, wine, and oregano and bring to the boil. Simmer uncovered for a further 2–3 minutes to reduce slightly. Remove from the heat, stir in the macaroni, and season to taste with salt and pepper.

4 Tip the mixture into an ovenproof dish and spread evenly. Mix the breadcrumbs with the Parmesan and butter, then spread over the top. Place the dish on a baking sheet and bake for 15–20 minutes, or until golden and bubbling, then serve at the table in the dish.

GOOD WITH A rocket or spinach side salad.

PREPARE AHEAD Prepare up to the end of step 3, then tip the mixture into the dish and top with the breadcrumb mixture. Cool, cover with foil, and chill for up to 8 hours. To serve, bake for 15 minutes, then remove the foil and bake for a further 10–15 minutes, or until thoroughly heated through and golden.

serves 4

prep 10 mins
• cook 20–25
mins

Pad Thai

This is one of Thailand's national dishes, where it is often served rolled up in a thin omelette.

INGREDIENTS

2 tbsp chopped coriander
1 red Thai chilli, deseeded
   and finely chopped
4 tbsp vegetable oil
250g (9oz) raw tiger prawns, peeled
4 shallots, finely chopped
1 tbsp sugar
4 large eggs, beaten
2 tbsp oyster sauce
1 tbsp Thai fish sauce
juice of 1 lime
350g (12oz) flat rice noodles, cooked
   according to packet instructions
250g (9oz) beansprouts
4 spring onions, sliced
115g (4oz) unsalted roasted peanuts,
   coarsely chopped
1 lime, cut into 4 wedges, to serve

METHOD

1 Mix together the coriander, chilli, and vegetable oil. Heat half the mixture in a wok, add the prawns, and stir-fry for 1 minute. Remove and set aside.

2 Add the remaining herb oil to the wok and stir-fry the shallots for 1 minute. Add the sugar and the eggs, and cook for 1 minute, stirring frequently to scramble the eggs as they begin to set.

3 Stir in the oyster sauce, fish sauce, lime juice, noodles, and beansprouts, and return the prawns to the wok. Stir-fry for 2 minutes, then add the spring onions and half the peanuts. Toss everything together for 1–2 minutes, or until piping hot.

4 To serve, divide between 4 individual bowls, scatter the remaining peanuts on top, and add a lime wedge.

GOOD WITH A fresh salad of beansprouts and shredded carrot, tossed with lime juice.

serves 4

prep 20 mins
• cook 10 mins

Vegetable curry

In Indian cooking, cardamom, cloves, coriander, and cumin seeds are all considered "warming spices" that heat the body from within, making this an excellent winter dish.

INGREDIENTS

4 tbsp ghee or sunflower oil

300g (10oz) waxy potatoes, diced

5 green cardamom pods, cracked

3 cloves

1 cinnamon stick, broken in half

2 tsp cumin seeds

1 onion, finely chopped

2 tsp fresh root ginger, peeled and grated

2 large garlic cloves, crushed

$1\frac{1}{2}$ tsp turmeric

1 tsp ground coriander

salt and freshly ground black pepper

400g can chopped tomatoes

pinch of sugar

2 carrots, peeled and diced

2 green chillies, deseeded (optional) and sliced

150g ($5\frac{1}{2}$oz) Savoy cabbage or green cabbage, sliced

150g ($5\frac{1}{2}$oz) cauliflower florets

150g ($5\frac{1}{2}$oz) peas

2 tbsp chopped coriander leaves

almond flakes, toasted, to garnish

METHOD

1 Melt the ghee or heat the oil in a large deep-sided frying pan over a high heat. Add the potatoes and stir-fry for 5 minutes, or until golden brown. Remove from the pan with a slotted spoon and set aside to drain on kitchen paper.

2 Reduce the heat to medium, add the cardamom pods, cloves, cinnamon, and cumin seeds, stirring just until the seeds begin to crackle. Add the onion and continue stir-frying for 5–8 minutes, or until softened. Add the ginger, garlic, turmeric, and ground coriander, then season to taste with salt and pepper and stir for 1 minute.

3 Stir in the tomatoes and sugar. Return the potatoes to the pan, add the carrots, chillies, and 250ml (8fl oz) water, and bring to the boil, stirring often. Reduce the heat to low and simmer for 15 minutes, or until the carrots are just tender, stirring occasionally. Add a little water, if needed.

4 Stir in the cabbage, cauliflower, and peas, and increase the heat to medium. Let the liquid gently bubble for a further 5–10 minutes, or until all the vegetables are tender. Stir in the coriander and adjust the seasoning, if necessary. Remove and discard the cardamom pods and cloves. Transfer to a serving bowl and sprinkle with almond flakes.

GOOD WITH Lots of freshly boiled basmati rice, or naan bread.

PREPARE AHEAD The whole dish can be cooked 1 day in advance and reheated; if it is too thick, stir in a little extra water.

serves 4–6

prep 20 mins
• cook 35–45 mins

freeze for up to 3 months

Kedgeree

This Anglo-Indian dish is traditionally made with just smoked haddock, but this version also includes salmon for added colour, texture, and flavour.

INGREDIENTS
300g (10oz) undyed smoked haddock
300g (10oz) salmon fillets
200g (7oz) basmati rice
pinch of saffron threads
60g (2oz) butter
4 eggs, hard boiled
salt and freshly ground black pepper
2 tbsp chopped parsley,
    plus extra to garnish
1 lemon, cut into wedges

METHOD
1 Place the fish in a single layer in a large frying pan. Pour over enough water to cover and heat gently to simmering point. Simmer for 5 minutes, then drain.

2 Meanwhile, cook the rice in boiling, salted water with a few saffron threads for 10–12 minutes, or according to packet instructions. When the rice is cooked, drain and stir in the butter.

3 Flake the fish into large chunks and add them to the rice. Discard the skin and bones.

4 Remove the yolks from the hard boiled eggs and reserve. Chop the egg whites and stir into the rice. Add the chopped parsley, and season to taste with salt and pepper.

5 Divide the mixture between heated plates and crumble the reserved egg yolks across the top with more chopped parsley. Serve garnished with lemon wedges.

GOOD WITH Triangles of buttered wholemeal toast.

serves 4

prep 20 mins
• cook 20 mins

Vegetable biryani

A curry that both vegetarians and meat eaters will enjoy.

INGREDIENTS

350g (12oz) basmati rice
1 large carrot, sliced
2 potatoes, peeled and cut into small pieces
1/2 cauliflower, cut into small florets
3 tbsp vegetable oil
1 red onion, chopped
1 red pepper, deseeded and chopped
1 green pepper, deseeded and chopped
1 courgette, chopped
85g (3oz) frozen peas
1 tsp turmeric
1 tsp mild chilli powder
2 tsp ground coriander
2 tsp mild curry paste
1 tsp cumin seeds
150ml (5fl oz) vegetable stock
60g (2oz) cashew nuts, lightly toasted

METHOD

1 In a large pan of simmering water, cook the rice for 10 minutes, or until just tender. Drain and set aside.

2 Cook the carrot and potatoes in a pan of boiling water for 5 minutes, or until almost tender. Add the cauliflower and cook until the vegetables are tender. Drain.

3 Heat the oil in a large frying pan, add the onion, and fry over a medium-low heat until softened. Add the red and green peppers and the courgette, and fry for 5 minutes, stirring occasionally.

4 Add the boiled vegetables and frozen peas, then stir in the turmeric, chilli powder, coriander, curry paste, and cumin seeds. Fry for a further 5 minutes, then add the stock, stirring. Preheat the oven to 180°C (350°F/Gas 4).

5 Spoon half the rice into an ovenproof dish and spread the vegetable mixture on top. Cover with the rest of the rice, cover with foil, and bake for 30 minutes, or until hot. Scatter over the cashews, and serve.

GOOD WITH Naan bread, mango chutney, lime pickle, or raita.

serves 4

prep 30 mins
• cook 45 mins

low fat

Sweet and sour prawns

Prawns stir-fried in a fragrant sauce spiked with chilli, garlic, and ginger make a deliciously different main course.

INGREDIENTS

3 tbsp rice wine vinegar
2 tbsp clear honey
1 tbsp caster sugar
2 tbsp light soy sauce
2 tbsp tomato ketchup
2 tbsp vegetable oil
3 shallots, peeled and sliced
2cm (³⁄₄in) piece of fresh root ginger,
   peeled and grated
1 red chilli, deseeded and finely chopped
1 garlic clove, crushed
1 small carrot, cut into matchsticks
1 celery stick, cut into matchsticks
1 green pepper, deseeded and cut into strips
500g (1lb 2oz) raw tiger prawns,
   peeled and deveined
2 spring onions, sliced lengthways, to garnish

METHOD

1 Heat the first 5 ingredients together in a small saucepan, until the honey and sugar melt. Remove from the heat and set aside.

2 Heat the oil in the wok, add the shallots, ginger, chilli, garlic, carrot, celery, and green pepper and stir-fry for 4 minutes.

3 Add the prawns and stir-fry for a further 2 minutes or until the prawns turn pink. Pour in the vinegar-and-sugar mixture and stir-fry for 1 minute, or until the prawns and vegetables are coated and everything is heated through.

4 To serve, transfer to a platter and garnish with spring onions.

GOOD WITH Boiled rice.

PREPARE AHEAD Step 1 can be completed several hours in advance.

serves 4

prep 20 mins
• cook 10 mins

wok

Shrimp diabolo

This quick and easy dish of prawns in a spicy tomato sauce makes a simple weeknight supper.

INGREDIENTS

2 tbsp olive oil
1 onion, chopped
1 red pepper, deseeded and sliced
3 garlic cloves, crushed
120ml (4fl oz) dry white wine or stock
250ml (8fl oz) passata (sieved tomatoes)
450g (1lb) cooked peeled tiger prawns,
    thawed if frozen
1–2 tbsp chilli sauce
2 tsp Worcestershire sauce

METHOD

1 Heat the oil in a large saucepan and fry the onion for 5 minutes, or until softened and beginning to turn golden. Add the pepper and fry for another 5 minutes, or until softened.

2 Add the garlic and fry for a few seconds. Stir in the wine and let it bubble away for 1–2 minutes.

3 Stir in the passata and bring to the boil, stirring, then reduce the heat and simmer for 5 minutes, or until reduced slightly.

4 Add the prawns and stir until piping hot. Do not overcook or the prawns will become tough. Stir in the chilli and Worcestershire sauces, and serve immediately.

GOOD WITH Boiled rice.

PREPARE AHEAD The sauce can be prepared up to 2 hours in advance. Add the prawns just before serving.

serves 4

prep 5 mins
• cook 20 mins

Seafood and tomato stew

This rustic stew is delicious any time of the day.

INGREDIENTS
2 tbsp olive oil
2 shallots, finely chopped
1 celery stick, finely chopped
2 garlic cloves, chopped
2 anchovies, rinsed
pinch of crushed chilli
salt and freshly ground black pepper
300ml can chopped tomatoes
250ml (8fl oz) white wine
200ml (7fl oz) fish stock or vegetable stock
400g (14oz) mix raw prawns, scallops, and monkfish
zest and juice of 1 lemon
1 tsp small capers, drained and rinsed

METHOD
1 Heat the oil in a saucepan. Add the shallots, celery, garlic, anchovies, and chilli. Season to taste with salt and pepper, and cook gently for 5 minutes, stirring.

2 Add the tomatoes, wine, and stock. Cook over a medium heat for 15–25 minutes, or until the sauce reduces slightly. Add the prawns, scallops, and monkfish, lemon zest and juice, and capers. Cook the shellfish for 5 minutes, or until the prawns are just pink.

GOOD WITH Toasted ciabatta.

serves 4

prep 10 mins
• cook 30 mins

Cod in tomato sauce

The tomatoes and wine add sweetness to this Spanish dish.

INGREDIENTS
2 tbsp olive oil
1kg (2¼lb) skinless cod fillet,
    cut into 4 pieces
1 large onion, finely sliced
1 garlic clove, finely chopped
4 large plum tomatoes, skinned,
    deseeded, and chopped
2 tsp tomato purée
1 tsp sugar
300ml (10fl oz) fish stock
120ml (4fl oz) dry white wine
2 tbsp chopped parsley
salt and freshly ground black pepper

METHOD
1 Preheat the oven to 200°C (400°F/Gas 6). Heat the oil in a casserole large enough to accommodate the cod in 1 layer. Fry the fish, skin-side down, over a medium-high heat, for 1 minute, or until the skin is crisp. Turn over and cook for 1 further minute. Remove with a slotted spoon and set aside.

2 Add the onions and garlic to the casserole and fry over a medium heat for 4–5 minutes, or until softened, stirring frequently. Add the tomatoes, tomato purée, sugar, stock, and wine, bring to a simmer, and cook, stirring, for 10–12 minutes.

3 Place the fish on top of the sauce and bake for 5 minutes. Remove from the oven, lift out the cod, and keep warm.

4 Place the casserole over a medium-high heat and allow the sauce to bubble for 3–4 minutes, until reduced and thickened. Stir in half the parsley and season to taste with salt and pepper. Divide the sauce between 4 warm plates and place a piece of fish on top. Serve at once, sprinkled with the remaining parsley.

serves 4

prep 10 mins
• cook 30 mins

large
flameproof
casserole

Chicken paprikash

Spicy paprika adds both flavour and colour to this hearty stew from Hungary.

INGREDIENTS

2 tbsp sunflower oil
2 small red onions, sliced
1 garlic clove, finely chopped
1 tbsp sweet paprika
¼ tsp caraway seeds
8 chicken thighs
250ml (8fl oz) hot chicken stock
1 tbsp red wine vinegar
1 tbsp tomato purée
1 tsp sugar
salt and freshly ground black pepper
250g (9oz) cherry tomatoes
chopped flat-leaf parsley, to garnish
soured cream, to serve

METHOD

1 Heat the oil in the casserole over a medium heat. Add the onion, garlic, paprika, and caraway seeds and fry, stirring, for about 5 minutes, or until the onions are softened. Use a slotted spoon to remove the ingredients from the pan and set aside.

2 Add the chicken thighs, skin-side down, to any oil remaining in the pan and fry for 3 minutes, then turn over and continue frying for a further 2 minutes. Return the onions and spices to the pan.

3 Mix together the stock, vinegar, tomato purée, sugar, and salt and pepper to taste. Pour over the chicken and bring to the boil, then reduce the heat to low, cover, and leave to simmer for 25 minutes, or until the chicken is tender.

4 Add the cherry tomatoes and shake the casserole vigorously to mix them into the sauce. Cover and simmer for a further 5 minutes. Sprinkle with parsley and serve with soured cream on the side.

GOOD WITH Creamy mashed potatoes or buttered noodles.

PREPARE AHEAD Steps 1 and 2 can be prepared up to 2 days in advance. Reheat until the chicken is piping hot.

serves 4

prep 10 mins
• cook 40–45 mins

large flameproof
casserole

freeze, without
the parsley or
soured cream,
for up to
1 month;
thaw at room
temperature

Creamy tarragon chicken

Fresh tarragon and cream is a classic pairing in French cuisine.

INGREDIENTS

30g (1oz) butter
1 tbsp rapeseed oil
4 chicken breasts, on the bone
250g (9oz) shallots, sliced
1 tsp dried *herbes de Provence*
2 garlic cloves, finely chopped
salt and freshly ground black pepper
250ml (8fl oz) hot chicken stock
120ml (4fl oz) dry white wine
250g (9oz) crème fraîche
2 tbsp chopped tarragon,
    plus extra sprigs to garnish

METHOD

1 Melt the butter with the oil in the casserole over a medium-high heat. Add the chicken breasts, skin-side down, and fry for 3 minutes, or until golden brown, then turn over and continue browning for a further 2 minutes.

2 Keep the chicken breasts skin-side up, then sprinkle with the shallots, dried herbs, garlic, and salt and pepper to taste. Add the stock and wine and bring to the boil. Reduce the heat to low, cover the casserole and leave to simmer for 25 minutes, or until the chicken is tender and the juices run clear when pierced with a knife. Lift out the chicken and set aside, then boil the sauce until it is reduced by about half.

3 Stir in the crème fraîche and chopped tarragon, and continue cooking until thickened. If the sauce becomes too thick, add more chicken stock; adjust the seasoning, if necessary. Serve the chicken sliced off the bone, coated with the sauce and garnished with tarragon sprigs.

GOOD WITH Boiled long-grain rice, or try it with mashed potatoes with olive oil, black pepper, and chopped pitted black olives.

PREPARE AHEAD Steps 1 and 2 can be prepared up to 2 days in advance and kept in a covered container in the fridge. Reheat, making sure the chicken is completely heated through before stirring in the crème fraîche.

serves 4

prep 10 mins
• cook 35 mins

large flameproof
casserole

freeze the dish
after step 2,
once cooled
completely, for
up to 1 month;
thaw at room
temperature,
then complete
the recipe

Chicken casserole with herb dumplings

This hearty winter casserole is a main meal in itself, but is especially good when served with freshly steamed greens.

INGREDIENTS

1 tbsp plain flour
salt and freshly ground black pepper
8 chicken thighs and drumsticks
2 tbsp olive oil
2 carrots, sliced
2 leeks, sliced
2 celery sticks, sliced
½ swede, diced
500ml (16fl oz) chicken stock
2 tbsp Worcestershire sauce

For the dumplings

125g (4½oz) self-raising flour
60g (2oz) light suet, shredded
1 tbsp parsley, chopped
1 tsp dried mixed herbs
salt and freshly ground black pepper

METHOD

1 Season the flour with salt and pepper. Toss the chicken pieces in the flour to coat. Heat half the oil in the casserole and fry the chicken, turning often, for 6 minutes, or until brown all over. Remove and keep warm. Pour the fat from the pan.

2 Add the remaining oil, carrots, leeks, celery, and swede to the casserole, and stir over the heat for 3–4 minutes to colour lightly. Return the chicken to the casserole, and add the stock and Worcestershire sauce. Bring to the boil, then reduce the heat, cover, and simmer for 20 minutes.

3 Meanwhile, to make the dumplings, place the flour in a bowl and stir in the suet, parsley, and dried herbs, and season to taste with salt and pepper. Stir in 5–6 tbsp cold water, or just enough to make a soft, not sticky, dough. With lightly floured hands, divide into 12 balls.

4 Remove the casserole lid and arrange the dumplings over the top. Cover and simmer for a further 20 minutes, or until the dumplings are risen and fluffy. Serve in the casserole.

serves 4

prep 15 mins
• cook 50 mins

large flameproof
casserole

freeze, without
dumplings, for
up to 3 months

Pot-roast guinea fowl with cabbage and walnuts

Guinea fowl cooked this way are moist and packed with flavour, as all the tasty juices are sealed within the pot.

INGREDIENTS

2 guinea fowls, about 1.25kg (2¾lb) each
salt and freshly ground black pepper
30g (1oz) butter
2 tbsp olive oil
1 small onion, finely chopped
1 leek, thinly sliced
2 celery sticks, sliced
100g (3½oz) smoked streaky
   bacon rashers, diced
85g (3oz) walnuts, halved
1 small Savoy cabbage, about 400g (14oz)
100ml (3½fl oz) hot chicken stock

METHOD

1 Preheat the oven to 200°C (400°F/Gas 6). Season the guinea fowl with salt and pepper.

2 Melt the butter with half the oil in the casserole, and fry the guinea fowls on a medium heat for 10 minutes, turning to brown on all sides. Remove from the heat and lift out the birds.

3 Add the remaining oil to the pan with the onion, leek, celery, and bacon, and fry, stirring, for 2–3 minutes, or until lightly coloured. Add the walnuts, then place the guinea fowl back on top of the fried vegetables.

4 Cut the cabbage into 8 wedges, leaving the leaves attached to the core. Tuck them loosely into the pot. Pour over the hot stock and season lightly. Bring to the boil, then cover and cook in the oven for 40–45 minutes, or until the vegetables are tender and the guinea fowl juices run clear when pierced.

5 Leave to stand for about 10 minutes before serving. To serve, remove the guinea fowls and cut each one in half. Arrange on plates and serve with vegetables and stock straight from the casserole.

serves 4

prep 20 mins
• cook 1 hr

large, deep
flameproof
casserole

Hoppin' John

This is a traditional dish from the American South.

INGREDIENTS

1 smoked ham hock, 1.1kg (2$\frac{1}{4}$lb)
1 fresh bouquet garni of celery,
  thyme sprigs, and 1 bay leaf
2 large onions, chopped
1 dried red chilli, chopped (optional)
1 tbsp groundnut oil or sunflower oil
200g (7oz) long-grain rice
2 x 400g cans black-eyed beans,
  drained and rinsed
salt and freshly ground black pepper
hot pepper sauce, to serve

METHOD

1 Put the ham hock in a saucepan, cover with cold water, and set over a high heat. Slowly bring to the boil, skimming the surface as necessary. Reduce the heat to low, add the bouquet garni, half the onions, and the chilli, then re-cover the pan and leave to simmer for 2$\frac{1}{2}$–3 hours, or until the meat is very tender when pierced with a knife.

2 Place a colander over a large heatproof bowl and strain the cooking liquid. Reserve the liquid and set the ham hock aside to cool.

3 Heat the oil in the casserole over a medium heat. Add the remaining onion and fry for 5 minutes, or until softened but not coloured, stirring occasionally. Add the rice and stir.

4 Stir in 450ml (15fl oz) of the reserved cooking liquid and the black-eyed beans. Season to taste with salt and pepper. Bring to the boil, then reduce the heat to low, cover tightly, and simmer for 20 minutes, without lifting the lid.

5 Meanwhile, remove the meat from the bone and cut into large chunks.

6 Remove the casserole from the heat and leave to stand for 5 minutes without lifting the lid. Using a fork, stir in the ham. Serve with a bottle of hot pepper sauce on the side.

PREPARE AHEAD Step 1 can be prepared 1 day in advance. Chill the meat until ready to use.

serves 4

prep 12 mins
• cook 3–3$\frac{1}{2}$ hrs

flameproof
casserole with
fitted lid

Chilli con carne

This Tex-Mex classic makes a colourful family supper. Serve it with bowls of other flavourful dishes so everyone can help themselves.

INGREDIENTS

1 tbsp olive oil
1 onion, thinly sliced
2 tbsp chilli sauce
1 garlic clove, crushed
1 tsp ground cumin
675g (1½lb) minced beef
400g can red kidney beans,
   drained and rinsed
400g can chopped tomatoes
salt and freshly ground black pepper
soured cream, to serve

METHOD

1 Heat the oil in a large saucepan over a medium heat. Add the onions and fry for 5 minutes, or until softened. Stir in the chilli sauce, garlic, cumin, and beef, and fry for 3 minutes, or until the meat browns, stirring occasionally.

2 Stir in the kidney beans and tomatoes and bring to the boil. Reduce the heat, cover, and leave to simmer for 40 minutes, stirring occasionally. Season to taste with salt and pepper and serve with the soured cream.

GOOD WITH Rice or nachos, and bowls of guacamole and salsa.

serves 4–6

prep 5 mins
• cook 50 mins

freeze for up to
3 months

Roast lamb with flageolets

A perfect Sunday lunch; the beans make a tasty change to the more traditional accompaniment of roast potatoes.

INGREDIENTS
½ leg of lamb, about 1.35kg (3lb)
2–3 sprigs rosemary
1 tbsp olive oil
salt and freshly ground black pepper
4 garlic cloves, roughly chopped
250g (9oz) baby plum tomatoes, halved
410g can flageolet beans, drained
1 tbsp tomato purée
150ml (5fl oz) dry white wine

METHOD
1 Preheat the oven to 180°C (350°F/Gas 4). With a small, sharp knife, make several deep cuts into the skin surface of the lamb. Push a few rosemary leaves into each cut. Place the lamb in a roasting tin, brush with oil, and season with salt and pepper. Roast for 1 hour.

2 Mix the remaining rosemary with the garlic, tomatoes, and flageolets. Remove the lamb from the oven and spoon the tomato and bean mixture around it. Mix the tomato purée with the wine and pour over the lamb.

3 Cover loosely with foil, then return to the oven for 30–40 minutes, or until the lamb is cooked but the juices are still slightly pink, stirring once. Allow the meat to rest for 10–15 minutes, loosely covered with foil, before carving.

PREPARE AHEAD The lamb can be prepared and stuffed with the rosemary leaves, ready for roasting, a few hours in advance of cooking.

serves 4

prep 15 mins
• cook 1 hr
40 mins

Lamb tagine with couscous

Dried apricots and orange juice, along with cumin, coriander, ginger, and thyme, give this the distinct flavour and aroma of Moroccan cuisine.

INGREDIENTS

1 onion, thinly sliced
1 tsp ground coriander
1 tsp ground cumin
1 tsp ground ginger
1 tsp dried thyme
2 tbsp sunflower oil or peanut oil
900g (2lb) boneless lamb, such as shoulder
   or chump steaks, cut into 2.5cm (1in) cubes
2 tbsp plain flour
300ml (10fl oz) orange juice
600ml (1 pint) chicken stock
120g (4oz) no-soak dried apricots
salt and freshly ground black pepper
mint leaves, to garnish

For the couscous
200g (7oz) quick-cook couscous
salt

serves 4

prep 10 mins,
plus marinating
• cook 1 hr
30 mins

large flameproof
casserole

freeze for up
to 1 month;
thaw over a low
heat and bring
to the boil
before serving

METHOD

1 Put the onion, coriander, cumin, ginger, thyme, and 1 tbsp of the oil in a large, non-metallic bowl, then mix in the lamb. Cover and refrigerate for at least 3 hours or overnight to marinate.

2 When ready to cook, preheat the oven to 160°C (325°F/Gas 3). Put the flour in a small bowl and slowly stir in the orange juice until smooth, then set aside.

3 Heat the remaining oil in the casserole over a high heat. Add the lamb mixture and fry, stirring frequently, for 5 minutes, or until browned.

4 Stir the flour mixture into the casserole with the stock. Bring to the boil, stirring, then remove the casserole from the heat, cover, and place in the oven for 1 hour.

5 Remove the casserole from the oven. Stir in the apricots, re-cover, and return to the oven. Cook for a further 20 minutes, or until the lamb is tender.

6 Meanwhile, put the couscous with salt to taste in a large heatproof bowl and pour over 2.5cm (1in) of boiling water. Cover with a folded tea towel and leave to stand for 10 minutes, or until the grains are tender. Fluff with a fork and keep warm. When the lamb is tender, taste and adjust the seasoning. Sprinkle with mint leaves and serve with the hot couscous.

PREPARE AHEAD The dish can be cooked up to 2 days in advance.

Braised lamb

This dish packs plenty of flavour with its tomato, olive, and herb sauce.

INGREDIENTS
900g (2lb) lamb leg, sliced
1 large onion, peeled
2 garlic cloves, peeled
1 fresh red chilli or ½ tsp dried
   chopped chilli
4 tbsp olive oil
120ml (4fl oz) red wine
115g (4oz) good quality black olives, pitted
400g can tomatoes
15g fresh thyme or 1 tsp dried thyme
salt and freshly ground black pepper
thyme or parsley, to garnish

METHOD
1 Cut each slice of lamb in half. Place the onion, garlic, and chilli in a food processor and pulse to a coarse paste. Heat the olive oil in the casserole and brown the meat on both sides, in batches if necessary.

2 Remove the lamb to a plate and gently fry the onion mixture for 5 minutes, stirring. Return the lamb to the pan, add the red wine, olives, tomatoes, and thyme and simmer, covered for 1 hour.

3 Check the lamb and simmer uncovered for half an hour, or until the lamb is tender. Season to taste with salt and pepper and garnish with freshly chopped herbs.

GOOD WITH Hot, fluffy couscous (see page 19.)

PREPARE AHEAD The dish can be prepared up to 3 days in advance. Take the dish out of the refrigerator and allow it to come to room temperature, then reheat for 30 minutes, or until piping hot.

serves 6

prep 20 mins
• cook 1½ hrs

large flameproof
casserole
with a lid

freeze for up
to 1 month

Navarin of lamb

This classic French stew is a complete one-pot meal, traditionally made with young spring vegetables.

INGREDIENTS

15g (½oz) butter

1 tbsp olive oil

900g (2lb) middle neck of lamb,
    cut into pieces

2 small onions, quartered

1 tbsp plain flour

400ml (14fl oz) lamb stock or beef stock

2 tbsp tomato purée

1 bouquet garni

salt and freshly ground black pepper

300g (10oz) small new potatoes

300g (10oz) small whole carrots

300g (10oz) baby turnips

175g (6oz) French beans

METHOD

1 Melt the butter with the oil in the casserole, add the lamb, and fry until brown on all sides. Add the onions and fry gently for 5 minutes, stirring frequently.

2 Sprinkle the flour over the meat and stir well for 2 minutes, or until the pieces are evenly coated. Stir in the stock, then add the tomato purée and bouquet garni, and season to taste with salt and pepper. Bring to the boil, then cover and simmer for 45 minutes.

3 Add the potatoes, carrots, and turnips. Cover and cook for a further 15 minutes, then stir in the beans, cover, and cook for a further 10–15 minutes, or until all the vegetables are tender.

GOOD WITH Chunks of French bread to soak up the juices.

PREPARE AHEAD Follow up to the end of step 2 the day before, then cool, cover, and refrigerate. Bring to the boil, add the vegetables, and continue following the recipe.

serves 4

prep 30 mins
• cook 1½ hrs

large flameproof
casserole

freeze for up to
3 months

Irish stew

There are many versions of this dish, with lamb and potatoes, cooked long and slow for maximum flavour and tenderness.

INGREDIENTS

8 best-end neck of lamb chops,
   about 750g (1lb 10oz) total weight
800g (1¾lb) onions, sliced
3 carrots, thickly sliced
800g (1¾lb) floury potatoes,
   peeled and thickly sliced
salt and freshly ground black pepper
large sprig of thyme
1 bay leaf
600ml (1 pint) lamb stock or beef stock

METHOD

1 Preheat the oven to 160°C (325°F/Gas 3).

2 Layer the lamb, onions, carrots, and a third of the potato slices in a large, heavy casserole. Season to taste with salt and pepper between the layers.

3 Tuck the thyme and bay leaf into the ingredients, then top with the remaining potato slices. Pour the stock over, cover, and place in the oven for 1 hour.

4 Remove the lid and return the casserole to the oven for a further 30–40 minutes, or until the top is browned. Serve hot.

GOOD WITH A fresh green vegetable, such as spring greens, kale, or broccoli.

PREPARE AHEAD The stew can be made the day before to the end of step 3. Reheat before serving.

serves 4–6

prep 20 mins
• cook 1 hr
40 mins

HEARTY

Thai red beef curry

Bird's-eye chillies in the curry paste make this dish truly fiery.

INGREDIENTS

450g (1lb) rump steak or sirloin,
   thinly sliced along the grain
1 large garlic clove, crushed
2–3 tbsp sunflower oil
½ onion, thinly sliced
1 red pepper, deseeded and thinly sliced
200g (7oz) button mushrooms, sliced
1½ tbsp Thai red curry paste
150g (5½oz) creamed coconut, dissolved
   in 450ml (15fl oz) boiling water
1½ tbsp Thai fish sauce
1 tbsp light soft brown sugar
100g (3½oz) spinach leaves,
   rinsed and shaken dry
30g (1oz) sweet basil leaves, torn

METHOD

1 Toss the beef and garlic in 1 tbsp of the oil. Heat a wok over a high heat, add the beef, and stir-fry for 1 minute, in batches if necessary, until the beef starts to change colour. Remove with a slotted spoon.

2 Add a little more oil to the wok, heat until shimmering, then stir-fry the onion and pepper for 2 minutes. Add the mushrooms and cook, stirring for 1–2 minutes, until all the vegetables are tender.

3 Stir in the curry paste, coconut, fish sauce, and sugar and bring to the boil, stirring. Reduce the heat, add the beef, spinach, and basil and cook for 3 minutes. Serve hot.

GOOD WITH Steamed rice.

serves 4

prep 20 mins
• cook 15 mins

110

Blanquette de veau

A simple, delicately flavoured stew with veal and a white sauce.

INGREDIENTS

675g (1½lb) veal shoulder or leg,
    boned, trimmed, and diced
2 onions, roughly chopped
2 carrots, peeled and chopped
squeeze of lemon juice
1 bouquet garni (6 parsley stalks, 1 bay leaf,
    1 celery stalk, 5 black peppercorns, and 3 fresh
    thyme sprigs, tied in muslin)
salt and freshly ground black pepper
85g (3oz) butter
18 white pearl onions
225g (8oz) brown cap mushrooms, quartered
2 tbsp plain white flour
1 egg yolk
2–3 tbsp single cream
fresh parsley, chopped, to garnish

METHOD

1 Put the veal, onions, carrots, lemon juice, and bouquet garni in the casserole with enough water to cover. Season with salt and pepper. Simmer over a low heat for 1 hour, or until the meat is tender.

2 Meanwhile, melt 25g (scant 1oz) of the butter in a frying pan over a medium heat. Add the onions and fry, stirring occasionally, until golden. Add another 25g (scant 1oz) of butter and the mushrooms. Fry for 5 minutes, or until soft, stirring occasionally.

3 Strain off the cooking liquid from the veal, reserving 600ml (1 pint). Add the meat and vegetables to the mushrooms and onions, then set aside, and keep warm.

4 Melt the remaining butter in a large pan. Add the flour and stir constantly for 1 minute. Remove the pan from the heat and gradually stir in the reserved liquid. Return the pan to the heat and bring the sauce to the boil, stirring, until it thickens.

5 Adjust the seasoning to taste, remove the pan from the heat, and let it cool slightly. Beat the egg yolk and cream in a small bowl, then slowly stir it into the sauce. Add the meat and vegetables and reheat, without boiling, for 5 minutes. Season, garnish with parsley, and serve.

GOOD WITH Steamed rice.

serves 4

prep 15 mins
• cook 1½ hrs

large
flameproof
casserole

Meat loaf

This recipe is great served hot for a weekday family meal, or cold in a packed lunch or sandwich.

INGREDIENTS

sunflower oil, for greasing
225g (8oz) lean minced beef
225g (8oz) minced pork
1 onion, finely chopped
4 tbsp fresh white breadcrumbs
salt and freshly ground black pepper
1 tsp paprika
2 tsp German mustard
2 tbsp chopped parsley
1 egg, beaten
3 hard-boiled eggs, peeled

For the sauce

1 tbsp capers, chopped
3 gherkins, chopped
1 tbsp finely chopped parsley
100g (3½oz) soured cream

METHOD

1 Preheat the oven to 200°C (400°F/Gas 6). Lightly oil the loaf tin.

2 Mix together the beef and pork, onion, breadcrumbs, salt and pepper, paprika, mustard, and parsley. Stir in the beaten egg.

3 Place half the mixture in the loaf tin, pressing to fill the base evenly. Arrange the hard-boiled eggs down the centre, then top with the remaining meat mixture, smoothing the top so that it is level.

4 Cover the tin with foil and bake in the oven for about 30 minutes, until firm. Leave the loaf to stand for 10 minutes before turning out on to a warmed plate.

5 Meanwhile, mix together the capers, gherkins, parsley, and soured cream.

6 Serve the meat loaf cut into slices, with the sauce spooned over and extra on the side.

GOOD WITH A salad of rocket and halved cherry tomatoes.

PREPARE AHEAD The meatloaf can be prepared up to the end of step 4, covered, and kept in the refrigerator until ready to bake for up to 3 days. The sauce can also be made up to 3 days in advance.

serves 4

prep 20 mins
• cook 30 mins

450g (1lb)
loaf tin

Watercress soup

Serve this velvety smooth soup hot, topped with shavings of Parmesan cheese.

INGREDIENTS
25g (scant 1oz) butter
1 onion, peeled and finely chopped
175g (6oz) watercress
3 ripe pears, cored and roughly chopped
1 litre (1¾ pints) vegetable stock
salt and freshly ground black pepper
200ml (7fl oz) double cream
juice of ½ lemon
Parmesan cheese, grated, to serve
olive oil, to drizzle

METHOD

1 Melt the butter in a saucepan and cook the onion for 10 minutes, or until soft, stirring occasionally to prevent burning.

2 Meanwhile, trim the watercress and pick off the leaves. Add the watercress stalks to the onion with the pears and stock, and season with salt and pepper.

3 Bring to the boil, cover, and simmer gently for 15 minutes. Remove from the heat and pour into a blender along with the watercress leaves. Process until the soup is a very smooth texture.

4 Stir in the cream and lemon juice, adjust the seasoning and serve sprinkled with Parmesan shavings and drizzled with a little oil.

PREPARE AHEAD The soup can be made up to 4 hours in advance and refrigerated until ready to use.

serves 4

prep 10 mins
• cook 15 mins

freeze the
soup, before
the cream is
added, for up
to 3 months

Stracciatella with pasta

This flavoursome soup makes a perfect light lunch.

INGREDIENTS

1.5 litres (2³/₄ pints) chicken stock
100g (3¹/₂oz) soup pasta
4 eggs
salt and freshly ground black pepper
¹/₂ tsp freshly grated nutmeg
2 tbsp grated Parmesan cheese
1 tbsp chopped parsley
1 tbsp olive oil

METHOD

1 Place the stock in a large pan and bring to the boil. Add the pasta and cook according to packet directions, or until *al dente*.

2 Break the eggs into a small bowl, add the nutmeg, season to taste with salt and pepper, and whisk lightly with a fork to break up the egg. Add the Parmesan and parsley.

3 Add the olive oil to the simmering stock, reduce the heat to low, then stir the stock lightly to create a gentle "whirlpool". Gradually pour in the eggs and cook for 1 minute, without boiling, so they set into fine strands. Leave to stand for 1 minute before serving.

serves 4–6

prep 10 mins
• cook 20 mins

Pasta alla carbonara

This is a popular Italian classic. Use the freshest eggs possible and serve the pasta straight after you've tossed it.

INGREDIENTS

450g (1lb) dried pasta, such as
    tagliatelle, spaghetti, or linguine
4 tbsp olive oil
175g (6oz) pancetta or cured unsmoked
    bacon rashers, rind removed,
    and finely chopped
2 garlic cloves, crushed
5 large eggs
75g (2½oz) Parmesan cheese, grated,
    plus extra to serve
75g (2½oz) pecorino cheese, grated,
    plus extra to serve
freshly ground black pepper
sprigs of thyme, to garnish

METHOD

1 Bring a large saucepan of salted water to the boil. Add the pasta, and bring to the boil for 10 minutes, or according to the packet instructions, until the pasta is *al dente*.

2 Meanwhile, heat half the oil in a large frying pan over a medium heat. Add the pancetta and garlic and fry, stirring, for 5–8 minutes, or until the pancetta is crispy.

3 Beat the eggs and cheeses together and season with black pepper. Drain the pasta well and return to the pan. Add the eggs, pancetta, and the remaining oil, and stir until the pasta is coated. Serve while still hot, sprinkled with the extra cheese and garnished with sprigs of thyme.

serves 4–6

prep 10 mins
• cook 10 mins

Singapore noodles

This popular dish combines the delicacy of Chinese cooking, the heat of Indian spices, and the fragrance of Malay herbs.

INGREDIENTS

2 tbsp vegetable oil

140g (5oz) skinless boneless
  chicken breasts,
  cut into thin strips

140g (5oz) raw prawns,
  peeled and deveined

1 onion, thinly sliced

$\frac{1}{2}$ red pepper, deseeded
  and cut into strips

1 head of pak choi, thinly sliced

2 garlic cloves, finely chopped

1 fresh red chilli, deseeded
  and finely chopped

115g (4oz) beansprouts

1 tbsp curry paste

2 tbsp light soy sauce

150g ($5\frac{1}{2}$oz) vermicelli egg noodles,
  cooked according to the packet instructions

2 large eggs, beaten

coriander, to garnish

serves 4

**prep 15 mins
• cook 10 mins**

low fat

**cook the prawns
on the day of
purchase**

wok

METHOD

1 Heat half the oil in the wok, add the chicken and stir-fry for 1 minute. Add the prawns and stir-fry for another 2 minutes. Remove them from the wok and set aside.

2 Add the rest of the oil to the wok and stir-fry the onion for 2 minutes, then add the pepper, pak choi, garlic, and chilli and cook for a further 2 minutes.

3 Tip in the beansprouts, stir-fry for 30 seconds, then stir in the curry paste, soy sauce, and stir-fry for 1 minute. Add the noodles, pour in the eggs, and toss everything together over the heat for 1 minute, or until the egg starts to set.

4 Return the chicken and prawns to the wok and stir-fry for 1 minute. Serve with the coriander scattered over.

PREPARE AHEAD On the day, slice the chicken, chop the vegetables, and prepare the prawns. Chill in separate bowls covered with cling film until ready to cook.

Quinoa tabbouleh

In this healthy salad, the quinoa has a creamy, nutty taste with a slight crunch once it is cooked.

INGREDIENTS

200g (7oz) quinoa
$^{1}/_{2}$ tsp salt
juice of 1 large lemon
250ml (8fl oz) olive oil
1 large cucumber, peeled,
    deseeded and chopped
1 large red onion, chopped
45g (1$^{1}/_{2}$oz) chopped parsley
45g (1$^{1}/_{2}$oz) chopped mint
115g (4oz) feta cheese, crumbled
100g (3$^{1}/_{2}$oz) Kalamata olives, pitted
salt and freshly ground black pepper

METHOD

1 Rinse the quinoa thoroughly in a fine mesh strainer. Drain and place it in a heavy pan. Heat, stirring constantly until the grains separate and begin to brown.

2 Add 600ml (1 pint) water and the salt and bring to the boil, stirring. Reduce the heat and cook for 15 minutes, or until the liquid is absorbed. Transfer to a bowl and set aside to cool.

3 Whisk together the lemon juice and 1 tbsp of the oil in a small bowl. Set aside.

4 Place the remaining oil, cucumber, onion, parsley, and mint in a separate, larger bowl. Add the quinoa and the lemon and oil dressing and toss. Sprinkle with the feta cheese and olives. Season to taste with salt and pepper.

serves 4

prep 10 mins
• cook 20 mins

Puy lentils with goat's cheese, olives, and fresh thyme

Small, grey-green Puy lentils are valued because of the way they hold their shape during cooking.

INGREDIENTS

350g (12oz) Puy lentils, rinsed
1 carrot, peeled and diced
1 shallot or small onion, finely chopped
2 sprigs of thyme
1 bay leaf
175g (6oz) black olives, pitted and chopped
85g (3oz) goat's cheese, rind removed if necessary,
   and crumbled
2 tbsp extra virgin olive oil
salt and freshly ground black pepper
salad leaves, to serve (optional)

METHOD

1 Place the lentils, carrot, shallot, thyme, and bay leaf in a saucepan with 1.2 litres (2 pints) of water. Simmer gently for 15–20 minutes or until the lentils are tender.

2 Drain the lentils well, transfer to a serving bowl and remove the bay leaf and thyme sprigs. Add the olives, goat's cheese, and olive oil and stir together. Season to taste with salt and pepper and serve warm.

GOOD WITH Grilled spicy sausages, lamb chops, or pork chops. For a vegetarian meal, serve with a salad of mixed green leaves.

PREPARE AHEAD The lentils can be cooked ahead in step 1 and gently reheated, or the whole dish can be assembled in advance and served chilled as a salad.

serves 4

prep 10 mins
• cook 30 mins

128

Piperade

This scrambled egg dish is from the Basque region of southwest France.

INGREDIENTS

2 tbsp olive oil
1 large onion, finely sliced or chopped
2 garlic cloves, crushed
1 red pepper, deseeded and chopped
1 green pepper, deseeded and chopped
85g (3oz) serrano ham
   or Bayonne ham, chopped
4 tomatoes, chopped
8 eggs, beaten
salt and freshly ground black pepper
2 tbsp chopped parsley, to garnish

METHOD

1 Heat the oil in a large frying pan and fry the onion over a gentle heat until softened. Add the garlic and peppers, and fry for 5 minutes, stirring occasionally.

2 Add the ham and cook for 2 minutes, then add the tomatoes and simmer for 2–3 minutes, or until any liquid has evaporated.

3 Pour the eggs into the pan and scramble, stirring frequently. Season to taste with salt and pepper, sprinkle with parsley, and serve.

serves 4

prep 5 mins
• cook 20 mins

Smoked haddock with spinach and pancetta

This deliciously satisfying dish is great for a quick supper.

INGREDIENTS

15g (¹⁄₂oz) butter, plus extra for greasing
1 tbsp olive oil
1 onion, finely chopped
100g (3¹⁄₂oz) pancetta or bacon, chopped
450g (1lb) spinach
100g (3¹⁄₂oz) crème fraîche
salt and freshly ground black pepper
75g (2¹⁄₂oz) Parmesan cheese, grated
800g (1³⁄₄lb) smoked fillets
   of haddock or cod, skinned
juice of ¹⁄₂ lemon
30g (1oz) fresh breadcrumbs

METHOD

1 Preheat the oven to 190°C (375°F/Gas 5) and butter an ovenproof serving dish. Melt the oil and butter together in a frying pan and fry the onion and pancetta for 5 minutes.

2 Add the spinach and stir until wilted, then stir in the crème fraîche, seasoning, and three-quarters of the Parmesan. Simmer until slightly thickened.

3 Spoon the spinach mixture into the ovenproof dish and place the fish on top. Sprinkle with lemon juice. Scatter with breadcrumbs and the remaining Parmesan, and bake for 15–20 minutes, or until the fish is cooked through and flakes easily.

PREPARE AHEAD Prepare up to 1 day in advance, and refrigerate until ready to cook.

serves 6

prep 10 mins
• cook 15–20
mins

Seafood curry

This quick curry is flavoured with chillies, coconut, and lime.

INGREDIENTS

600g (1lb 5oz) skinless boneless white fish,
  such as cod or haddock, cut into bite-sized
  pieces, rinsed and patted dry
$\frac{1}{2}$ tsp salt
$\frac{1}{2}$ tsp turmeric
$\frac{1}{2}$ onion, chopped
1cm ($\frac{1}{2}$in) piece fresh root ginger,
  peeled and coarsely chopped
1 garlic clove, crushed
2 tbsp sunflower oil
1 tsp black mustard seeds
4 green cardamom pods, crushed
2–4 dried red chillies, crushed
100g ($3\frac{1}{2}$oz) creamed coconut, dissolved
  in 500ml (16fl oz) boiling water
12 king prawns, peeled and deveined
2 tbsp fresh lime juice
freshly ground black pepper
coriander leaves, to garnish
lemon wedges, to garnish

METHOD

1 Put the fish in a non-metallic bowl, sprinkle over the salt and turmeric, and turn over so both sides are lightly covered. Set aside.

2 Put the onion, ginger, and garlic in a food processor or blender and process until it makes a paste. Heat a deep frying pan over a high heat until hot. Add the oil and swirl around, then reduce the heat to medium, add the onion paste, and fry, stirring, for 3–5 minutes, or until it just begins to colour. Stir in the mustard seeds, cardamom, and chillies and stir for 30 seconds.

3 Stir in the coconut mixture. Leave to bubble for 2 minutes, then reduce the heat to medium-low, add the fish pieces and any juices in the bowl, and spoon the sauce over the fish. Simmer for 2 minutes, spooning the sauce over the fish once or twice as it cooks, taking care not to break up the pieces.

4 Add the prawns to the pan and simmer for 2 minutes, or until they turn pink and the fish flakes easily. Add lime juice and season to taste with salt and pepper. Serve garnished with coriander leaves and lemon wedges.

serves 4

prep 15 mins
• cook 12 mins

Thai green chicken curry

By using a shop-bought jar of Thai curry paste, this flavoursome dish is very quick to prepare.

INGREDIENTS

1 tbsp olive oil
4 tsp shop-bought Thai red curry paste
    or green curry paste (use more
    paste for a spicier sauce)
4 skinless boneless chicken breasts,
    about 140g (5oz) each, cut into
    bite-sized pieces
2 tbsp light soy sauce
400ml can coconut milk
175g (6oz) open-cap mushrooms, chopped
6 spring onions, trimmed, with the green
    part cut into 5mm (1/4in) slices
salt and freshly ground black pepper
chopped coriander, to garnish

METHOD

1 Heat the oil in a large frying pan over a medium heat. Add the curry paste and stir. Add the chicken and stir-fry for 2 minutes, or until lightly browned.

2 Pour in the soy sauce and coconut milk and bring to the boil, stirring. Lower the heat, stir in the mushrooms and most of the spring onions, and season with salt and pepper to taste, then simmer for about 8 minutes, or until the chicken is tender and cooked through.

3 Serve hot, garnished with coriander and the remaining sliced spring onions.

GOOD WITH Boiled or steamed long-grain rice or plain noodles, as a starter or part of a Thai buffet.

PREPARE AHEAD Complete up to 24 hours in advance and reheat.

serves 4

prep 10 mins
• cook 10 mins

Devilled turkey

Serve these spicy stir-fried turkey strips as a healthy lunch or supper.

INGREDIENTS

2 tbsp wholegrain mustard
2 tbsp mango chutney
2 tbsp Worcestershire sauce
¼ tsp ground paprika
3 tbsp orange juice
1 red chilli, chopped (optional)
2 tbsp olive oil
450g (1lb) turkey breast escalope,
    cut into strips
1 onion, peeled and finely chopped
1 red pepper, cored and cut into strips
1 orange pepper, cored and cut into strips
1 garlic clove, crushed

METHOD

1 Mix the mustard, chutney, Worcestershire sauce, paprika, orange juice, and chilli, if using, together until well combined.

2 Heat the oil in a frying pan or wok, add the turkey, and cook over a high heat until browned. Remove the turkey from the pan and set aside, covered to keep it warm.

3 Add the onion to the pan and fry for 2–3 minutes, or until beginning to colour. Add the peppers and garlic and fry, stirring constantly, for 3–4 minutes, or until tender.

4 Stir in the mustard mixture and return the turkey to the pan. Cook for 5 minutes or until piping hot and the turkey is cooked through.

GOOD WITH Stir-fried spinach and rice or noodles.

serves 4

prep 10 mins
• cook 15 mins

Quick lamb curry

Use leftover lamb for this dish and adjust the amount of curry powder to your taste.

INGREDIENTS

1 onion, quartered
3 garlic cloves, sliced
2.5cm (1in) piece of fresh root ginger,
   peeled and chopped
2 green peppers, deseeded and quartered
1 green chilli, deseeded
2 tbsp oil
1 tbsp black mustard seeds
1–2 tbsp curry powder
400g can chopped tomatoes
100g (3$\frac{1}{2}$oz) creamed coconut
500g (1lb 2oz) cooked lamb,
   cut into bite-sized pieces
115g (4oz) frozen peas
salt and freshly ground black pepper
chopped coriander, to garnish

METHOD

1 Place the onions, garlic, ginger, green peppers, and chilli in a blender with 1 tbsp water and blend to a purée.

2 Heat 1 tbsp oil in a large saucepan or flameproof casserole, add the mustard seeds and fry, stirring, for 30 seconds, or until they begin to pop. Pour in the onion purée, increase the heat, and allow to bubble, stirring frequently, for 3–5 minutes, or until all the water has evaporated and the purée is thick and fairly dry.

3 Add the remaining oil and curry powder, and stir-fry for 30 seconds, then add the tomatoes with their juice, and 75ml (2$\frac{1}{2}$fl oz) water. Cook for 1 minute, stirring constantly, then add the coconut, and stir until well incorporated.

4 Add the lamb and peas and bring back to boiling point, then reduce the heat, cover, and simmer for 10–15 minutes, until heated through. Season to taste with salt and pepper, and serve garnished with chopped coriander.

GOOD WITH Rice or naan bread, or as part of a feast with other curries.

serves 4

prep 15 mins
• cook 25 mins

freeze for up
to 3 months

Chinese chilli beef stir-fry

This hot stir-fry is best when the meat has time to marinate. But for super quick results, first coat and fry.

INGREDIENTS

500g (1lb 2oz) rump steak,
    cut into thin strips
3 tbsp dark soy sauce
2 tbsp rice vinegar
1 tbsp Chinese five-spice powder
freshly ground black pepper
4 tbsp vegetable oil
1 large red chilli, deseeded and finely chopped
1 garlic clove, peeled and crushed
1 tsp grated, fresh root ginger
$\frac{1}{2}$ red pepper, deseeded and thinly sliced
100g (3$\frac{1}{2}$oz) mangetout, halved lengthways
100g (3$\frac{1}{2}$oz) tenderstem broccoli
1 tsp cornflour
115ml (4fl oz) beef stock
few drops of toasted sesame oil

METHOD

1 Put the strips of steak in a bowl with the soy sauce, rice vinegar, and five-spice powder, stirring until coated. Season with black pepper, cover the bowl with cling film, and, if possible, leave to marinate.

2 Heat half the oil in the wok, add the chilli, garlic, ginger, and red pepper, and stir-fry for 3 minutes. Add the mangetout and broccoli, and stir-fry for 2 minutes. Remove the vegetables and set aside.

3 Add the rest of the oil, drain the beef from the spicy liquid (reserving the liquid), and stir-fry over a high heat for 1 minute. Return the vegetables and add the spicy liquid. Stir the cornflour into the stock and gradually pour into the wok. Bring to the boil, stirring, for 1–2 minutes, or until piping hot.

4 Drizzle over the sesame oil, and serve at once with boiled rice or egg noodles.

serves 4

**prep 15 mins,
plus marinating
• cook 10 mins**

**low GI if served
with extra stir-fry
vegetables
rather than rice
or noodles**

wok

Soufflé omelette

This puffy omelette takes a little extra effort, but its lightness at the end makes it well worth making.

INGREDIENTS
2 eggs, separated
salt and freshly ground black pepper
15g (1/2oz) butter
30g (1oz) mature Cheddar cheese, grated
30g (1oz) Gruyère cheese, grated
30g (1oz) sliced ham, cut into strips
2–3 chopped chives

METHOD
1 Preheat the grill on its highest setting. Place the egg yolks in a small bowl and whisk until creamy. Season to taste with salt and pepper, add 2 tbsp water, and whisk again. Wash the whisk in hot soapy water and dry, then use to whisk the whites in a large, clean bowl, until they form soft peaks.

2 Melt the butter in a non-stick frying pan over a medium heat. Meanwhile, using a large metal spoon, quickly fold the egg yolks into the egg whites with half the cheese, taking care not to over-mix.

3 When the butter is foaming, pour the mixture into the pan, shaking the pan to make sure the mixture is evenly distributed. Cook the omelette for 1 minute, then slide the palette knife around the edge to loosen it from the pan. Scatter the omelette with the remaining cheese, and the ham, and place under the hot grill for 1 minute to allow the surface to cook.

4 Sprinkle the omelette with chives. To serve, slide the palette knife around the edge again, carefully fold the omelette in half, and slide on to a warmed plate.

GOOD WITH A rocket and watercress salad.

serves 1

prep 10 mins
• cook 5 mins

palette knife

Sauté of liver, bacon, and onions

Quick to cook, tender calves' liver is the perfect partner to salty bacon and is served here in a rich sauce.

INGREDIENTS

350g (12oz) calves' liver
200g (7oz) sweet-cured, smoked streaky
   bacon thin-cut rashers
1 tbsp olive oil
30g (1oz) unsalted butter
4 shallots, thinly sliced
120ml (4fl oz) vermouth
1 tsp Dijon mustard
dash of mushroom ketchup
   or Worcestershire sauce (optional)
salt and freshly ground black pepper

METHOD

1 Cut the liver and the bacon rashers into strips about 6cm (2$\frac{1}{4}$in) long and 1.5cm ($\frac{1}{2}$in) wide. Set aside.

2 Heat half the oil and half the butter in a frying pan over a medium heat, add the shallots, and fry, stirring frequently, for 5 minutes, or until soft and golden. Remove from the pan and reserve.

3 Add the remaining oil and butter to the pan and increase the heat to high. Add the liver and bacon and stir-fry for 3–4 minutes, until the liver is cooked but still slightly pink inside.

4 Return the shallots to the pan, pour in the vermouth, and let it bubble for 1–2 minutes, scraping any bits stuck to the bottom of the pan.

5 Reduce the heat to medium and stir in the mustard and the mushroom ketchup (if using). Serve at once.

GOOD WITH Smooth, creamy mashed potato and green beans for a tasty supper dish, or served on toasted bread croûtes for a quick dinner party starter.

serves 4

prep 10 mins
• cook 10 mins

Tomato soup

Easy to make, using canned tomatoes, this delicious soup can be enjoyed all year round.

INGREDIENTS

1 tbsp olive oil
1 onion, chopped
1 garlic clove, sliced
2 celery sticks, sliced
1 carrot, sliced
1 potato, chopped
2 x 400g cans tomatoes
750ml (1¼ pints) vegetable stock
   or chicken stock
1 bay leaf
1 tsp sugar
salt and freshly ground black pepper

METHOD

1 Heat the oil in a large saucepan over a medium-low heat, add the onion, garlic, and celery, and fry, stirring frequently, until softened but not coloured.

2 Add the carrot and potato and stir for 1 minute, then add the tomatoes with their juice, stock, bay leaf, and sugar. Season to taste with salt and pepper, bring to the boil, then reduce the heat, cover, and simmer for 45 minutes, or until the vegetables are very soft.

3 Remove from the heat and allow to cool slightly, then process in a blender or food processor until smooth, working in batches if necessary. Taste and adjust the seasoning, then reheat and serve.

PREPARE AHEAD Make the soup up to 48 hours in advance and reheat before serving.

serves 4

prep 20 mins
• cook 55 mins

low fat

Carrot and orange soup

A light, refreshing soup with a hint of spice, this is the perfect start to a summer meal.

INGREDIENTS

2 tsp light olive oil or sunflower oil
1 leek, sliced
500g (1lb 2oz) carrots, sliced
1 potato, about 115g (4oz), chopped
1/2 tsp ground coriander
pinch of ground cumin
300ml (10fl oz) orange juice
500ml (16fl oz) vegetable stock
    or chicken stock
1 bay leaf
salt and freshly ground black pepper
2 tbsp chopped coriander, to garnish

METHOD

1 Place the oil, leeks, and carrots in a large saucepan and cook over a low heat for 5 minutes, stirring frequently, or until the leeks have softened. Add the potato, coriander, and cumin, then pour in the orange juice and stock. Add the bay leaf and stir occasionally.

2 Increase the heat, bring the soup to the boil, then lower the heat, cover, and simmer for 40 minutes, or until the vegetables are very tender.

3 Allow the soup to cool slightly, then transfer to a blender or food processor and process, until smooth, working in batches if necessary.

4 Return to the saucepan and add a little extra stock or water if the soup is too thick. Bring back to a simmer, then transfer to heated serving bowls and sprinkle with the chopped coriander.

GOOD WITH A spoonful of low-fat plain yogurt, or a swirl of cream.

PREPARE AHEAD The soup can be made up to 2 days in advance and reheated before serving.

serves 4

prep 10 mins
• cook 40 mins

low fat

Lentil soup

This hearty vegetarian soup has just a touch of spice and is quick and easy to prepare.

INGREDIENTS

1 tbsp olive oil
2 onions, finely chopped
2 celery sticks, finely chopped
2 carrots, finely chopped
2 garlic cloves, crushed
1–2 tsp curry powder
150g (5½oz) red lentils
1.4 litres (2½ pints) vegetable stock
120ml (4fl oz) tomato juice or vegetable juice
salt and freshly ground black pepper

METHOD

1 Heat the oil in a large pan over a medium heat, then add the onions, celery, and carrots. Cook, stirring, for 5 minutes, or until the onions are soft and translucent.

2 Add the garlic and curry powder and cook, stirring, for a further 1 minute, then add the lentils, stock, and tomato juice.

3 Bring to the boil, then lower the heat, cover, and simmer for 25 minutes, or until the vegetables are tender. Season to taste with salt and pepper, and serve hot.

GOOD WITH A spoonful of natural yogurt and crusty bread.

serves 4

prep 20 mins
• cook 35 mins

low fat

Lentil salad with lemon and almonds

Puy lentils have a crisp taste when combined with the refreshing flavours of fragrant coriander and preserved lemon.

INGREDIENTS

400g (14oz) Puy (French) green lentils
2 preserved lemons, rinsed
    and cut into small dice
2 tbsp chopped coriander
2 spring onions, thinly sliced
3 tbsp red wine vinegar
100ml (3½fl oz) extra virgin olive oil
salt and freshly ground black pepper
4 tbsp flaked almonds, toasted
coriander leaves, to garnish

METHOD

1 Bring a large pan of water to the boil and add the lentils. Return to the boil, reduce the heat, cover, and simmer for 15–20 minutes, or until the lentils are just tender. Drain, then rinse quickly in cold water and drain well.

2 Place the lentils into a large bowl and stir in the diced lemons, chopped coriander, and half the spring onions. Whisk together the wine vinegar and oil, season to taste with salt and pepper, and stir into the lentils.

3 Cover the salad and leave to stand for 20 minutes to allow the flavours to develop.

4 Mix the almonds with the remaining spring onion and the coriander leaves, then scatter over the salad and toss lightly to serve.

GOOD WITH Grilled chicken or lamb chops, or with roasted white fish, such as cod or monkfish.

PREPARE AHEAD The salad can be prepared several hours in advance. Cover and refrigerate until required.

serves 4

prep 10 mins,
plus standing
• cook 15–20
mins

Kasha with vegetables

Kasha is a healthy and delicious wholegrain cereal that is prepared similarly to risotto. This makes a hearty vegetarian main course.

INGREDIENTS

2 tbsp olive oil
1 onion, finely chopped
1 carrot, finely chopped
1 garlic clove, finely chopped
2 flat mushrooms, sliced
1 celery stick, finely chopped
550g (1¼lb) kasha
120ml (4fl oz) dry white wine
1.2 litres (2 pints) hot vegetable
    stock or water
1 beetroot, steamed or roasted
    until tender, chopped
2 tbsp chopped parsley
60g (2oz) goat's cheese, crumbled

METHOD

1 Heat the oil in a large saucepan. Add the onion, carrot, garlic, mushrooms, and celery and sauté for 8–10 minutes, stirring frequently, until brown. Add the kasha and cook, stirring for another 2–3 minutes. Add the wine and continue stirring until all the liquid has been absorbed.

2 Gradually add the hot vegetable stock, 120ml (4fl oz) at a time, and stirring until it has been absorbed before adding more. Cook for about 20 minutes, or until the kasha is soft and chewy.

3 Toss in the chopped beetroot and remove from the heat. Serve with the parsley and the goat's cheese.

GOOD WITH Crusty bread, as a main meal.

serves 4

prep 10 mins
• cook 40 mins

Spaghetti mare e monti

The ingredients, as the name of this well-known pasta dish suggests, come from the sea and the mountains.

INGREDIENTS

15g (1/2oz) dried porcini mushrooms, rinsed
6 ripe plum tomatoes
2 tbsp extra virgin olive oil
150g (51/2oz) baby button mushrooms
2 garlic cloves, finely chopped
1 bay leaf
150ml (5fl oz) white wine
225g (8oz) cooked tiger prawns,
   defrosted if frozen
salt and freshly ground black pepper
400g (14oz) dried spaghetti

METHOD

1 Place the porcini in a bowl and pour 150ml (5fl oz) boiling water over. Leave to soak for 30 minutes. Remove the mushrooms with a slotted spoon and chop, then strain the soaking liquid through a fine sieve and reserve.

2 Meanwhile, put the tomatoes in a heatproof bowl. Make a small nick in the skin of each with the point of a sharp knife, then pour over enough boiling water to cover. Leave for 30 seconds, then drain, peel, deseed, and roughly chop (see page 14).

3 Heat the oil in a large frying pan. Add the porcini and button mushrooms and fry, stirring, until golden. Add the garlic and cook for 30 seconds. Pour in the reserved porcini soaking liquid, add the bay leaf, and simmer briskly until the liquid is reduced to a glaze. Reduce the heat to low.

4 Pour in the wine and tomatoes and simmer for 7–8 minutes, or until the liquid is slightly reduced and the tomatoes break down. Remove the bay leaf, add the prawns, and cook for 1 minute, or until heated through. Season to taste with salt and pepper.

5 Meanwhile, cook the spaghetti in plenty of lightly salted boiling water for 10 minutes, or as directed on the packet. Drain thoroughly, then return to the pan. Add the sauce, toss to combine, and serve immediately.

serves 4

prep 15 mins,
plus soaking
• cook 15 mins

low fat

160

Chilli tofu stir-fry

This quick and easy dish plays on tofu's ability to take on the flavour of other ingredients.

INGREDIENTS

2 tbsp sunflower oil
85g (3oz) unsalted cashew nuts
300g (10oz) firm tofu, cubed
1 red onion, thinly sliced
2 carrots, peeled and thinly sliced
1 red pepper, deseeded and chopped
1 celery stick, chopped
4 chestnut mushrooms, sliced
175g (6oz) beansprouts
2 tsp chilli sauce
2 tbsp light soy sauce
1 tsp cornflour
175ml (6fl oz) vegetable stock

METHOD

1 Heat the oil in the wok and add the cashews; stir-fry for 30 seconds, or until lightly browned. Drain and set aside.

2 Add the tofu and stir-fry until golden. Drain and set aside. Stir-fry the onion and carrots for 5 minutes, then add the pepper, celery, and mushrooms and stir-fry for 3–4 minutes. Finally, add the beansprouts and stir-fry for 2 minutes. Keep the heat under the wok high, so the vegetables fry quickly, without overcooking.

3 Return the cashews and tofu to the pan and drizzle in the chilli sauce. In a small bowl, mix the soy sauce with the cornflour and pour into the pan, along with the stock. Toss over the heat for 2–3 minutes, or until the sauce is bubbling.

GOOD WITH Boiled rice or Chinese-style egg noodles.

serves 4

prep 10 mins
• cook 15 mins

wok

Fideua

This Spanish pasta dish, with a tasty mixture of seafood, is hearty and filling.

INGREDIENTS

pinch of saffron threads
750ml (1¼ pints) hot fish stock
2–3 tbsp olive oil
1 onion, finely chopped
2 garlic cloves, crushed
3 ripe tomatoes, skinned,
    deseeded, and chopped
1 tsp sweet paprika or smoked paprika
300g (10oz) spaghetti or linguine,
    broken into 5cm (2in) lengths
225g (8oz) raw prawns, peeled and deveined
8 small scallops, cut in half
12 clams or mussels
225g (8oz) firm white fish, such as cod, haddock,
    or monkfish, cut into 2cm (¾in) pieces
140g (5oz) frozen peas
salt and freshly ground black pepper
2 tbsp chopped fresh parsley

METHOD

1 Put the saffron threads in a small bowl and add 2 tbsp of the hot fish stock. Set aside.

2 Heat the oil in a large frying pan or paella pan over a medium heat. Add the onion and garlic and fry for 5–8 minutes, or until soft and translucent, stirring frequently. Add the tomatoes and paprika and cook for a further 5 minutes. Add the saffron with its soaking liquid and half the remaining stock, increase the heat, and bring to the boil.

3 Add the spaghetti, reduce the heat, and simmer, uncovered, stirring occasionally for 5 minutes. Add the prawns, scallops, clams, white fish, and the peas, and cook for a further 5 minutes, or until the pasta and fish are cooked through. If the mixture begins to dry out too much, add a little more stock. Season to taste with salt and pepper, sprinkle with the parsley, and serve hot, straight from the pan.

GOOD WITH Aioli and chunks of crusty bread to mop up the juices.

serves 4

prep 15 mins
• cook 25 mins

low fat

Swordfish baked with herbs

Rosemary is not often used with fish, but it perfectly complements the strong flavours of this dish.

INGREDIENTS

4 swordfish steaks, about
   175g (6oz) each, skinned
freshly ground black pepper
2 tbsp extra virgin olive oil,
   plus extra for greasing
1 fennel bulb, thinly sliced
4 tomatoes, sliced
1 lemon, sliced
4 tbsp chopped flat-leaf parsley
1 tbsp chopped mint
4 sprigs of thyme
2 tsp chopped rosemary leaves
100ml (3½fl oz) dry white wine

METHOD

1 Preheat the oven to 180°C (350°F/Gas 4). Season the swordfish steaks with plenty of black pepper. Lightly grease an ovenproof dish with the oil and place the sliced fennel in an even layer in the dish.

2 Lay the fish in the dish in a single layer and top with the tomato and the lemon slices. Sprinkle with the parsley, mint, thyme, and rosemary, and pour the wine over the fish. Drizzle with the olive oil and cover the dish tightly with foil.

3 Bake for 15–20 minutes, or until the swordfish steaks are just cooked. Serve immediately, spooning the juices in the dish over the fish.

GOOD WITH Steamed new potatoes and green vegetables, such as broccoli or French beans.

serves 4

prep 20 mins
• cook 15–20 mins

low fat

Chicken and chickpea pilaf

This one-pot rice dish is full of flavour and is easy to make.

INGREDIENTS
pinch of saffron threads
2 tsp vegetable oil
6 skinless boneless chicken thighs,
   cut into small pieces
2 tsp ground coriander
1 tsp ground cumin
1 onion, sliced
1 red pepper, deseeded and chopped
2 garlic cloves, peeled and crushed
225g (8oz) long-grain rice
750ml (1¼ pints) hot chicken stock
2 bay leaves
400g can chickpeas, drained and rinsed
60g (2oz) sultanas
60g (2oz) flaked almonds
   or pine nuts, toasted
3 tbsp chopped flat-leaf parsley

METHOD
1 Crumble the saffron threads into a small bowl, add 2 tbsp boiling water, and set aside for at least 10 minutes.

2 Meanwhile, heat half the oil in a large saucepan, add the chicken, coriander, and cumin, and fry over a medium heat for 3 minutes, stirring frequently. Remove from the pan and set aside. Lower the heat, add the rest of the oil, the onion, pepper, and garlic, and fry for 5 minutes, or until softened.

3 Stir in the rice, return the chicken to the pan, and pour in about three-quarters of the stock. Add the bay leaves and saffron with its soaking water and bring to the boil. Simmer for 15 minutes, or until the rice is almost cooked, adding more stock as needed. Stir in the chickpeas and sultanas, and continue cooking until the rice is tender. Transfer to a warm serving platter and serve hot, sprinkled with the toasted nuts and chopped parsley.

serves 4

prep 20 mins
• cook 35 mins

low fat

Burgundy beef

In this classic French casserole, *Boeuf Bourguignon*, long, slow braising ensures the meat becomes tender.

INGREDIENTS

175g (6oz) streaky bacon rashers, chopped
1–2 tbsp oil
900g (2lb) braising steak,
    cut into 4cm (1½in) cubes
12 small shallots
1 tbsp plain flour
300ml (10fl oz) red wine
300ml (10fl oz) beef stock
115g (4oz) button mushrooms
1 bay leaf
1 tsp dried *herbes de Provence*
salt and freshly ground black pepper
4 tbsp fresh parsley, chopped

METHOD

1 Preheat the oven to 160°C (325°F/Gas 3). Fry the bacon in a non-stick frying pan until lightly browned. Drain on kitchen paper and transfer into a casserole.

2 Depending on how much fat is left from the bacon, add a little oil to the pan if necessary so that you have about 2–3 tbsp. Fry the beef in batches over a high heat, transferring to the casserole as they brown.

3 Reduce the heat to a medium heat and fry the shallots. Transfer to the casserole and stir the flour into the remaining fat in the frying pan. If the pan is quite dry, mix the flour with a little of the wine or stock. Pour the wine and stock into the frying pan and bring to the boil, stirring constantly until smooth.

4 Add the mushrooms, bay leaf, and dried herbs. Season to taste with salt and pepper and pour the contents of the pan over the meat and shallots in the casserole. Cover and cook in the oven for 2 hours, or until the meat is very tender.

5 Serve hot, sprinkled with chopped parsley.

GOOD WITH Mashed potatoes, baby carrots, and a green vegetable such as broccoli or French beans.

PREPARE AHEAD This dish can be prepared ahead and reheated in a 180°C (350°F/Gas 4) oven for 30 minutes when ready to serve.

serves 4

prep 25 mins
• cook 2½ hours

low GI

freeze for up to
3 months

Arroz con pollo

This is a colourful chicken and rice dish from Latin America.

INGREDIENTS

2 tbsp olive oil
8 chicken thighs
1 Spanish onion, finely sliced
1 green pepper, deseeded and chopped
1 red pepper, deseeded and chopped
2 garlic cloves, finely chopped
1 tsp smoked paprika
1 bay leaf
230g can chopped tomatoes
1 tsp thyme leaves
1 tsp dried oregano
175g (6oz) long-grain rice
pinch of saffron threads
750ml (1¼ pints) chicken stock
2 tbsp tomato purée
juice of ½ lemon
salt and freshly ground black pepper
100g (3½oz) frozen peas

METHOD

1 Preheat the oven to 180°C (350°F/Gas 4). Heat half the oil in the casserole and fry the chicken thighs over high heat, turning frequently, or until evenly browned. Remove from the casserole, drain, and set aside.

2 Add the remaining oil, reduce the heat and fry the onion until softened. Add the chopped peppers and garlic and fry for 5 minutes, or until they start to soften. Add the paprika, bay leaf, tomatoes, thyme, and oregano, and stir in the rice. Fry for 1–2 minutes, stirring constantly.

3 Crumble in the saffron, add the stock, tomato purée, and lemon juice, and season to taste with salt and pepper.

4 Return the chicken thighs to the casserole, pushing them down into the rice, cover, and cook in the oven for 15 minutes. Add the peas and return to the oven for a further 10 minutes, or until the rice is tender and has absorbed the cooking liquid. Serve hot, straight from the casserole.

serves 4

prep 20 mins
• cook 45 mins

low fat

large
flameproof
casserole

172

Chicken fricassée

This is a classic one-pot French dish in which chicken is simmered until the meat falls off the bone.

INGREDIENTS

2 tbsp olive oil
2 tbsp plain flour
salt and freshly ground black pepper
4 chicken legs, divided into drumstick
   and thigh, skin removed
115g (4oz) button mushrooms
4 shallots, sliced
2 garlic cloves, crushed
4 waxy potatoes, peeled and cut
   into small pieces
2 tsp finely chopped rosemary leaves
150ml (5fl oz) dry white wine
300ml (10fl oz) chicken stock
1 bay leaf

METHOD

1 Heat the oil in a large deep casserole. Season the flour with salt and pepper. Dust the chicken pieces with the flour and fry over a medium-high heat until golden brown, turning often. Remove from the pan and set aside.

2 Slice the mushrooms. Add the shallots to the pan and fry for 2–3 minutes, stirring often. Add the garlic, mushrooms, potatoes, and rosemary, and fry for 2 minutes.

3 Pour in the wine and bring to the boil. Allow to bubble and reduce for 1 minute, then pour in the stock, and bring to the boil. Return the chicken to the pan, add the bay leaf, and cover tightly. Reduce the heat and cook gently for 45 minutes, or until the chicken is very tender. Discard the bay leaf and adjust the seasoning, if necessary. Serve hot.

serves 4

prep 15 mins
• cook 1 hr
15 mins

low fat

174

Rabbit Provençale

A French bistro dish that makes the most of this healthy
and easy-to-cook meat.

INGREDIENTS

2 tbsp olive oil
1.25kg (2¾lb) rabbit, cut into 10 pieces
100g (3½oz) pancetta, chopped
1 onion, chopped
4 garlic cloves, finely chopped
sprig of rosemary, plus extra to garnish
3 sage leaves
900g (2lb) tomatoes, skinned and crushed
salt and freshly ground black pepper
150ml (5fl oz) dry white wine
200ml (7fl oz) boiling water

METHOD

1 Heat the oil in the casserole over a medium-high heat and fry the rabbit pieces for 10 minutes, or until browned on all sides. Remove from the pan and drain on kitchen paper. Pour off most of the fat remaining in the pan.

2 Add the pancetta and onion to the pan and cook, stirring, for 5 minutes, or until the pancetta is browned and the onion softened. Add the garlic, stir for 30 seconds, then add the rosemary, sage, and tomatoes, and season to taste with salt and pepper. Cook, stirring frequently, for 10 minutes, or until the tomatoes begin to break up and thicken.

3 Return the rabbit to the pan and add the wine. Stir together and cook over a medium-high heat for 20 minutes, or until the liquid has reduced slightly and the sauce is quite thick. Stir in the boiling water, and add more salt and pepper, if desired. Partially cover, reduce the heat, and simmer, stirring occasionally, for 10–20 minutes, or until the rabbit is very tender.

4 Remove from the heat and rest for at least 10 minutes. Serve, garnished with rosemary.

GOOD WITH Boiled new potatoes and broccoli.

serves 4–6

prep 15 mins,
plus resting
• cook 1 hr
15 mins

flameproof
casserole

Bouillabaisse

Originally nothing more than a humble fisherman's soup using the remains of the day's catch, bouillabaisse has evolved into one of the great Provençal dishes.

INGREDIENTS

4 tbsp olive oil
1 onion, thinly sliced
2 leeks, thinly sliced
1 small fennel bulb, thinly sliced
2–3 garlic cloves, finely chopped
4 tomatoes, skinned, deseeded, and chopped
1 tbsp tomato purée
250ml (8fl oz) dry white wine
1.5 litres (2³/₄ pints) fish stock
   or chicken stock
pinch of saffron threads
strip of orange zest
1 bouquet garni
salt and freshly ground black pepper

1.35kg (3lb) mixed white and oily fish
   and shellfish, such as gurnard, John Dory,
   monkfish, red mullet, prawns, and mussels,
   heads and bones removed
2 tbsp Pernod
8 thin slices day-old French bread,
   toasted, to serve

For the rouille

125g (4¹/₂oz) mayonnaise
1 bird's-eye chilli, deseeded and roughly chopped
4 garlic cloves, roughly chopped
1 tbsp tomato purée
¹/₂ tsp salt

METHOD

1 Heat the oil in a large saucepan over a medium heat. Add the onion, leeks, fennel, and garlic and fry, stirring frequently, for 5–8 minutes, or until the vegetables are softened but not coloured. Add the tomatoes, tomato purée, and wine and stir until blended.

2 Add the stock, saffron, orange zest, and bouquet garni. Season to taste with salt and pepper, and bring to the boil. Reduce the heat, partially cover the pan, and simmer for 30 minutes, or until the soup is reduced slightly, stirring occasionally.

3 To make the rouille, place all ingredients into a blender or food processor and process until smooth. Transfer to a bowl, cover with cling film, and chill until required.

4 Just before the liquid finishes simmering, cut the fish into chunks. Remove the orange zest and bouquet garni from the soup and add the firm fish. Reduce the heat to low and let the soup simmer for 5 minutes, then add the delicate fish and simmer for a further 2–3 minutes, or until all the fish is cooked through and flakes easily. Stir in the Pernod, and season to taste with salt and pepper.

5 To serve, spread each piece of toast with rouille and put 2 slices in the bottom of each bowl. Ladle the soup on top and serve.

GOOD WITH Thick slices of lightly toasted crunchy French bread.

PREPARE AHEAD Make the rouille up to 2 days in advance, cover, and chill.

serves 4

prep 20 mins
• cook 45 mins

tap the mussels
and discard
any that do
not close

181

Fisherman's tuna stew

This fish stew, which Basque fisherman call *marmitako de bonito*, was originally made at sea to provide for a hungry crew.

INGREDIENTS

900g (2lb) potatoes
750g (1lb 10oz) fresh tuna
350g (12oz) jar roasted red peppers
3 tbsp olive oil
1 large onion, finely sliced
2 garlic cloves, crushed
1 bay leaf
salt and freshly ground pepper
400g (14oz) can chopped tomatoes
300g (10oz) frozen petits pois
2 tbsp chopped parsley

METHOD

1 Peel the potatoes and cut into thick rounds. Cut the tuna into pieces roughly the same size as the potatoes, and slice the peppers into strips.

2 Heat the oil in a casserole, stir in the onion, garlic, and bay leaf, and cook, stirring, until the onions are translucent. Add the potatoes, stir well, season to taste with salt and pepper, then cover with water. Boil for 10 minutes, or until the potatoes are almost cooked, then add the tomatoes, and continue to cook for a further 5 minutes.

3 Reduce the heat to low, add the tuna, and cook for a further 5 minutes, then add the petits pois and the peppers, and cook very gently for 10 minutes. Sprinkle with parsley to serve.

serves 4

prep 10 mins
• cook 35 mins

Mediterranean lasagne

A simple baked vegetarian pasta dish full of Italian flavours.

INGREDIENTS

For the tomato sauce
4 tbsp sunflower oil
1 onion, chopped
1 garlic clove, chopped
4 tbsp tomato purée
4 x 400g cans chopped tomatoes
8 basil leaves, torn
salt and freshly ground black pepper

For the lasagne
6 baby aubergines, halved lengthways
1 large red pepper, deseeded and sliced
2 large flat mushrooms, cut into chunks
375g pack fresh lasagne sheets
350g (12oz) mozzarella cheese, thinly sliced
225g (8oz) ricotta cheese
4 tbsp grated Parmesan cheese

METHOD

1 To make the sauce, heat the oil in a large saucepan over medium heat. Add the onion and garlic and fry, stirring occasionally, for 5–8 minutes, or until soft and golden.

2 Stir in the tomato purée, the tomatoes with their juice, half the basil leaves, and salt and pepper to taste. Lower the heat and simmer, uncovered, for 20 minutes, or until the sauce has thickened. Stir in the remaining basil leaves.

3 Preheat the oven to 190°C (375°F/Gas 5) and heat the grill to High. Grill the aubergine, pepper, and mushrooms for 5–10 minutes, or until they are softened but still hold their shape. Season to taste with salt and pepper.

4 Briefly drop each pasta sheet in a bowl of lukewarm water, then drain. Lightly oil the ovenproof dish and spoon in a ladleful of the tomato sauce. Top with a layer of pasta, some vegetables, another ladleful of sauce, then some of the mozzarella and ricotta. Repeat the layers, finishing with tomato sauce (you may not need it all), topped with some vegetables. Sprinkle with the Parmesan cheese.

5 Cover the dish with oiled aluminium foil. It's important that the dish is tightly sealed so the pasta continues cooking without drying out. Bake for 30–40 minutes.

6 Remove the foil, return the dish to the oven, and bake for 15 minutes, or until the top is golden and the sauce bubbles around the edge of the dish. Allow to stand for 10 minutes before serving.

GOOD WITH Garlic bread and a green salad.

PREPARE AHEAD Assemble the lasagne up to 24 hours in advance and keep chilled. Add an extra 10–15 minutes to the cooking time.

serves 4

prep 25 mins
• cook 1 hr
40 mins

20 x 15cm
(8 x 6in) shallow
ovenproof dish

Vegetable moussaka

Lentils replace the lamb and yogurt is a light alternative to béchamel sauce in this vegetarian version of a Greek favourite.

INGREDIENTS

2 aubergines, about 600g
(1lb 5oz) in total, cut into
1cm (½in) slices
2 courgettes, thickly sliced
2 onions, thickly sliced
2 red peppers, cored, deseeded,
and thickly sliced
4 tbsp olive oil
salt and freshly ground black pepper
2 garlic cloves, coarsely chopped

1 tbsp chopped thyme leaves
400g can chopped tomatoes
300g can green lentils,
drained and rinsed
2 tbsp chopped flat-leaf parsley
2 eggs, lightly beaten
300g (10oz) Greek-style yogurt
pinch of paprika
85g (3oz) feta cheese, crumbled
2 tbsp white sesame seeds

METHOD

1 Preheat the oven to 220°C (425°F/Gas 7). Place the aubergine, courgettes, onions, and red peppers into a roasting tin. Drizzle over the olive oil, toss together to coat the vegetables evenly, then season to taste with salt and pepper.

2 Roast for 10 minutes, toss, add the garlic and thyme, and roast for a further 30–35 minutes, or until the vegetables are tender. Reduce the temperature to 180°C (350°F/Gas 4).

3 Stir the tomatoes with their juices, the lentils, and the parsley into the roast vegetables. Taste and adjust the seasoning, if necessary. Transfer the vegetables to a 23cm (9in) square ovenproof serving dish.

4 Beat the eggs and yogurt with the paprika, and season to taste with salt and pepper. Spread the mixture over the vegetables, and sprinkle the feta cheese on top. Put the dish on a baking sheet and bake for 40 minutes. Sprinkle with the sesame seeds and bake for 10 minutes, or until the top is golden. Leave to stand for at least 2 minutes, then serve while still warm.

GOOD WITH A mixed green salad on the side, and crusty country-style bread for mopping up the juices.

serves 4–6

prep 20 mins
• cook 1 hr
30 mins

Paella

This Spanish rice dish has many regional variations. This version, *Paella Marinera*, contains a delicious mix of seafood.

INGREDIENTS

1.2 litres (2 pints) hot fish stock
large pinch of saffron threads
2 tbsp olive oil
1 onion, finely chopped
2 garlic cloves, crushed
2 large tomatoes, skinned and diced
12 king prawns, peeled
225g (8oz) squid, sliced into rings
400g (14oz) paella rice
85g (3oz) petit pois
4 langoustines or Dublin Bay prawns
12–16 mussels, cleaned
1 tbsp chopped parsley, to garnish

METHOD

1 Pour a little of the hot fish stock into a cup or jug, add the saffron threads, and set aside to infuse. Heat the oil in a paella pan or large frying pan, and fry the onion and garlic until softened. Add the tomatoes and cook for 2 minutes, then add prawns and squid and fry for 1–2 minutes, or until the prawns turn pink.

2 Stir in the rice, then stir in the saffron liquid, petit pois, and 900ml (1½ pints) of stock. Simmer, uncovered, without stirring, over a low heat for 12–14 minutes, or until the stock has evaporated and the rice is just tender, adding a little extra stock if necessary.

3 Meanwhile, cook the langoustines in 150ml (5fl oz) simmering stock for 3–4 minutes, or until cooked through. Transfer to a warm plate with a slotted spoon. Add the mussels to the stock, cover, and cook over a high heat for 2–3 minutes, or until open. Remove from the pan with a slotted spoon, discarding any that have not opened.

4 Reserve 8 mussels for garnish. Remove the rest from their shells and stir into the paella. Arrange the reserved mussels and langoustines on top, and garnish with parsley.

serves 4

prep 10 mins
• cook 30 mins

**tap the mussels
and discard
any that do
not close**

188

Moules marinières

The title of this classic French recipe for mussels cooked in wine, garlic, and herbs means "in the style of the fisherman".

INGREDIENTS

60g (2oz) butter
2 onions, finely chopped
3.6kg (8lb) fresh mussels, cleaned
2 garlic cloves, crushed
600ml (1 pint) dry white wine
4 bay leaves
2 sprigs of thyme
salt and freshly ground black pepper
2–4 tbsp chopped parsley

METHOD

1 Melt the butter in a very large heavy saucepan, add the onion, and fry gently until lightly browned. Add the mussels, garlic, wine, bay leaves, and thyme, and season to taste with salt and pepper. Cover, bring to the boil, and cook for 5–6 minutes, or until the mussels have opened, shaking the pan frequently. If you do not have a large enough saucepan for all the mussels, cook them in 2 pans instead.

2 Remove the open mussels with a slotted spoon, discarding any that remain closed. Transfer the mussels to warmed bowls, cover, and keep warm.

3 Strain the liquid into a pan and bring to the boil. Season to taste with salt and pepper, add the parsley, pour it over the mussels, and serve at once.

GOOD WITH Plenty of French bread for mopping up the juices.

serves 4

prep 15 mins
• cook 10 mins

tap the mussels
and discard
any that do
not close

Tiger prawns with chilli and cheese

A quick-to-prepare supper to serve for friends.

INGREDIENTS

600g (1lb 5oz) raw tiger prawns, peeled
juice of 2 limes
few drops of Tabasco sauce
2 tbsp olive oil
2 red onions, finely sliced
3 red chillies, deseeded and
   finely chopped
3 garlic cloves, crushed
salt and freshly ground black pepper
250ml (8fl oz) double cream
85g (3oz) Gruyère cheese or
   Parmesan cheese, grated

METHOD

1 Put the prawns in a large bowl, toss in the lime juice and Tabasco sauce, cover, and leave to marinate in the refrigerator for 30 minutes.

2 Preheat the grill on its highest setting. Heat the oil in frying pan and lightly fry the onions for 5 minutes before adding the chillies and garlic. Continue to cook for another 5 minutes.

3 Put the onion mixture into the serving dish. Drain the prawns, spread over the onions, then season to taste with salt and pepper. Pour the cream over the prawns and sprinkle with the grated cheese.

4 Place under the grill and cook for 5–6 minutes, or until the prawns turn pink and the cheese is golden brown and bubbling. Serve at once.

GOOD WITH Fresh bread and a crisp green salad.

serves 6

prep 10 mins,
plus marinating
• cook 15–16 mins

large flameproof
serving dish

Fish coconut stew

This popular Brazilian stew is called *Moqueca de Peixe*. The palm oil (*dendê*) lends a distinctive flavour as well as an orange colour, but you can use a lighter oil or leave it out altogether.

INGREDIENTS

4 tbsp olive oil

1 onion, thinly sliced

3 ripe tomatoes, skinned, deseeded, and chopped

1 red pepper, deseeded and thinly sliced

1 green pepper, deseeded and thinly sliced

salt and freshly ground black pepper

300ml (10fl oz) coconut milk

3 tsp tomato purée

800g (1¾lb) white fish, cut into large chunks or strips

3 tbsp palm oil (optional)

1 tbsp chopped coriander leaves

For the chilli salsa

1 ripe tomato, skinned, deseeded, and chopped

1 small red onion, finely chopped

1 garlic clove, finely chopped

1 tbsp red wine vinegar

1 tbsp lime juice

1 tbsp sunflower oil

1 tbsp chopped flat-leaf parsley

1 tsp chilli sauce

METHOD

1 Heat the oil in a deep frying pan over medium heat. Add the onion and fry, stirring frequently, for 5 minutes, or until soft but not coloured. Add the tomatoes and the red and green peppers, lower the heat, and simmer, stirring from time to time, for 20 minutes, or until the vegetables have softened. Season to taste with salt and pepper, stir in the coconut milk and tomato purée, and bring back to the boil.

2 Meanwhile, make the chilli salsa. Mix all the ingredients together and place in a serving bowl.

3 Add the fish to the vegetables in the pan and cook, stirring occasionally, for 5–10 minutes, according to the size of the pieces of fish, until just cooked through. Do not overcook. Stir in the palm oil, if using.

4 Transfer the stew to a serving dish and scatter with coriander. Serve with the salsa alongside.

GOOD WITH Boiled white rice.

PREPARE AHEAD Make the stew up to the end of step 1 the day before and chill. The salsa also can be made up to 24 hours in advance, stirring in the parsley at the last minute.

serves 4

prep 15 mins
• cook 35 mins

Salt cod braised with vegetables

In this dish, known in Spain as *Bacalao a la cazuela*, salt cod is tender and fragrant with the classic Spanish aromas of garlic, bay leaves, and saffron.

INGREDIENTS

3 tbsp olive oil
1 onion, finely diced
white parts of 2 leeks, finely sliced
3 garlic cloves, minced
3 tomatoes, peeled, deseeded, and chopped
500g (1lb 2oz) potatoes, diced
salt and freshly ground black pepper
2 bay leaves
large pinch of saffron threads
800g (1¾lb) thick-cut bacalao (salt cod),
    soaked and cut into 4 pieces
120ml (4fl oz) dry white wine
2 tbsp chopped parsley

METHOD

1 Heat the oil in a large, shallow, heatproof casserole. Add the onion and leek, and fry gently, stirring constantly for 5 minutes, or until soft.

2 Add the garlic and tomatoes, and cook for a further 2 minutes, stirring continuously. Add the potatoes, season to taste with salt and pepper, and add the bay leaves and saffron.

3 Add the bacalao, skin-side up, on top of the vegetables. Pour in the wine, plus 250ml (8fl oz) water, then bring gently to a simmer and cook for 25–30 minutes. Shake the casserole once or twice every 5 minutes to help release gelatine from the fish to thicken the sauce.

4 Sprinkle over the chopped parsley, and serve straight from the casserole.

serves 4

prep 20 mins, plus soaking • cook 40 mins

soak the fish for at least 24 hrs in enough water to cover it, changing the water 2–3 times to remove saltiness of the brine

Mussels with tomatoes and chilli

This dish allows the warm Mediterranean aroma of smoked paprika to add its own special flavour to mussels.

INGREDIENTS
2 tbsp extra virgin olive oil
30g (1oz) unsalted butter
2 shallots, finely chopped
½ tsp smoked paprika
1 celery stick, finely chopped
1 garlic clove, crushed
1 large red chilli, deseeded
    and finely chopped
1.8kg (4lb) mussels
2 tomatoes, chopped
90ml (3fl oz) dry white wine
2 tbsp chopped flat-leaf parsley

METHOD
1 Heat the oil and butter in a large, deep saucepan with a tight-fitting lid. Add the shallots, smoked paprika, celery, garlic, and chilli, and fry over a low heat until the shallots have softened.

2 Add the mussels, tomatoes, and wine, stir well, and increase the heat to medium-high. Cover and cook for 2–3 minutes, or until the mussels have opened. Discard any that remain closed.

3 Transfer the mussels to deep serving bowls and sprinkle with parsley. Serve at once.

GOOD WITH Thin-cut chips or pieces of warm crusty bread to mop up the rich juices.

serves 4

prep 15 mins
• cook 10 mins

tap the mussels
and discard
any that do
not close

Baked bream

This classic Iberian dish, *Besugo al Horno*, combines fish and potatoes.

INGREDIENTS

2 sea bream, 600g (1lb 5oz) each
1 tbsp tapenade
2 lemon slices, thickly sliced
juice of 1 lemon
3 tbsp olive oil
675g (1½lb) potatoes, very thinly sliced
1 onion, thinly sliced
2 peppers, deseeded and sliced into thin rings
4 garlic cloves, chopped
2 tbsp chopped parsley
1 tsp hot paprika (pimentón picante)
120ml (4fl oz) dry white wine
salt and freshly ground black pepper

METHOD

1 Make 2 diagonal cuts on each side of the thickest part of both fish. Place in a non-metallic dish and spread the tapenade over the inside and outside of each fish. Tuck a lemon slice into the gills of each fish, drizzle with the lemon juice, and place in the refrigerator to marinate for 1 hour.

2 Preheat the oven to 190°C (375°F/Gas 5). Grease an ovenproof dish with 1 tbsp of the olive oil. Layer half the potatoes in the dish, then the onion and peppers on top. Scatter with the garlic and parsley, and sprinkle with the paprika, before layering the remaining potatoes on top. Drizzle over the remaining olive oil, and sprinkle with 2–3 tbsp of water. Cover with foil and bake for 40 minutes, or until the potatoes are cooked and golden.

3 Increase the temperature to 220°C (425°F/Gas 7). Place the fish on top of the potatoes, pour over the wine, season with salt and pepper, and return to the oven, uncovered, for 20 minutes, or until the fish is cooked. Serve immediately.

PREPARE AHEAD The fish can be prepared to the end of step 1 and marinated up to 6 hours in advance, then covered and chilled.

serves 4

prep 10 mins,
plus marinating
• cook 1 hr

Lobster thermidor

This irresistibly indulgent seafood dish is thought to be named in honour of a play called *Thermidor* that opened in 1894 in Paris.

INGREDIENTS

2 cooked lobsters, about 675g (1½lb) each
paprika, to sprinkle
lemon wedges, to serve

For the sauce

30g (1oz) butter
2 shallots, finely chopped
120ml (4fl oz) white wine
120ml (4fl oz) fish stock
150ml (5fl oz) double cream
½ tsp made English mustard
1 tbsp lemon juice
2 tbsp parsley, chopped
2 tsp tarragon, chopped
salt and freshly ground black pepper
75g (2½oz) Gruyère cheese, grated

METHOD

1 Cut the lobsters in half lengthways. Remove the meat from the claws and tail, along with any coral or meat from the head. Cut the meat into bite-sized pieces. Clean out the shells and reserve.

2 To prepare the sauce, melt the butter in a small saucepan, add the shallots, and fry gently until softened but not browned. Add the wine and boil for 2–3 minutes, or until the liquid is reduced by half.

3 Add the stock and cream and boil rapidly, stirring, until reduced and slightly thickened. Stir in the mustard, lemon juice, and herbs, then season to taste with salt and pepper. Stir in half the cheese.

4 Preheat the grill on its highest setting. Add the lobster meat to the sauce, then divide between the lobster shells. Top with the remaining cheese.

5 Place the lobsters on a foil-lined grill pan and grill for 2–3 minutes, or until bubbling and golden. Sprinkle with a little paprika and serve hot, with lemon wedges.

serves 4

prep 25 mins
• cook 20 mins

Chicken gumbo

Traditionally made with seafood in Louisiana, this version is made with chicken instead.

INGREDIENTS

1 tbsp sunflower oil
1 onion, chopped
2 celery sticks, chopped
1 green pepper, deseeded and chopped
1 garlic clove, chopped
450g (1lb) skinless boneless
   chicken breasts, cubed
$\frac{1}{2}$ tsp dried oregano
2 tsp hot paprika
$\frac{1}{2}$ tsp ground cumin
1 tbsp plain flour
115g (4oz) spicy sausage,
   such as chorizo, sliced
400g can chopped tomatoes
450ml (15fl oz) chicken stock
225g (8oz) frozen sliced okra,
   or baby courgettes, sliced

METHOD

1 Heat the oil in a large saucepan and fry the onion, celery, and pepper over a medium heat for 5 minutes, or until softened, stirring frequently. Add the garlic and fry for a further few seconds.

2 Add the chicken and fry, turning, until evenly browned. Sprinkle with the oregano, paprika, cumin, and flour. Stir well and cook for 1 minute, then add the sausage, tomatoes, and stock.

3 Bring to the boil, stirring frequently, then reduce the heat and simmer for 20 minutes. Add the okra, return to simmering point, and let cook for a further 20 minutes.

serves 4

prep 20 mins
• cook 50 mins

Grilled quail with ginger glaze

These quail have a sweet-sour, spicy glaze that's very moreish. Cook them on a barbecue, under a grill, or on a hot griddle pan.

INGREDIENTS

8 quail
limes wedges, to serve

For the glaze

1 garlic clove, crushed
1 tbsp finely grated, fresh root ginger
3 tbsp sweet chilli dipping sauce
juice of 1 lime
1 tbsp sesame oil
3 tbsp finely chopped coriander

METHOD

1 Using kitchen scissors, cut each quail along the backbone, from the neck end to the parson's nose. Open each quail, place on to a cutting board, skin-side up, and press firmly with your hand to flatten. Slash the breast skin a couple of times with a knife to ensure even cooking.

2 Mix the glaze ingredients together with a fork. Brush evenly over each quail, pressing into the cuts, and leave to marinate in the fridge for at least an hour or overnight.

3 Preheat a grill to hot. Grill the quail on a foil-lined grill pan, turning once, for 12–15 minutes, or until golden brown and the juices show no trace of pink when pierced.

4 Serve hot, with lime wedges for squeezing.

GOOD WITH Boiled rice and green vegetables, such as French beans.

PREPARE AHEAD Prepare steps 1 and 2, then cover and refrigerate for up to 2 days.

serves 4

prep 15 mins,
plus marinating
• cook 15 mins

freeze the quail
in the marinade
for up to
1 month

Beef strogonoff

This classic Russian dish was named after the Strogonov family.

INGREDIENTS

675g (1½lb) fillet steak, or rump,
    or sirloin, trimmed
3 tbsp plain flour
salt and freshly ground black pepper
1 tbsp paprika, plus extra for sprinkling
50g (1⅓oz) butter or 4 tbsp olive oil
1 onion, thinly sliced
225g (8oz) chestnut mushrooms, sliced
300ml (10fl oz) soured cream
    or crème fraîche
1 tbsp French mustard
lemon juice

METHOD

1 Thinly slice the steak into 5cm (2in) strips. Season the flour with salt, pepper, and paprika then coat the beef strips in the flour. Heat a deep frying pan, put in half the butter, add the onion, and fry over a low heat for 8–10 minutes, or until soft and golden. Add the mushrooms and fry for a few minutes, or until just soft.

2 Remove the onions and mushrooms and keep warm. Increase the heat and, when the pan is hot, add the remaining butter, put in the beef strips, and fry briskly, stirring, for 3–4 minutes.

3 Return the onions and mushrooms to the pan and season to taste with salt and pepper. Shake the pan over the heat for 1 minute.

4 Lower the heat, stir in the cream and mustard, and cook gently for 1 minute; do not allow the cream to come to the boil.

5 Add lemon juice to taste and serve immediately.

GOOD WITH Rice or tagliatelle.

serves 4

prep 15 mins
• cook 25 mins

Daube of beef with wild mushrooms

This rich stew benefits from being made a few days before serving so the flavours can develop.

INGREDIENTS

2 tbsp olive oil
30g (1oz) butter
2 tbsp plain flour
salt and freshly ground black pepper
900g (2lb) chuck steak,
    cut into 7.5cm (3in) pieces
115g (4oz) rindless bacon rashers, chopped
2 small onions, finely chopped
3 garlic cloves, crushed
1 celery stalk, finely chopped
3 carrots, diced
1 tbsp chopped fresh or dry thyme
900ml (1½ pints) red wine
2 tbsp brandy (optional)
zest and juice of 1 orange
175g (6oz) field mushrooms
30g (1oz) dried mushrooms
1 tbsp tomato purée

METHOD

1 Heat the olive oil and butter in the casserole. Season the flour with salt and pepper. Coat the meat in the seasoned flour, then brown on all sides in the casserole. Remove the pieces to a warm plate.

2 Fry the bacon, onions, garlic, and celery in the casserole, until lightly coloured. Stir in the beef along with the carrots and thyme. Pour in the red wine, the brandy, and the orange zest and juice; bring to the boil, stirring, then reduce the heat, cover, and simmer for 1 hour.

3 Clean and slice the field mushrooms. Put the dried mushrooms in a bowl and pour over boiling water. Leave to soak for 15 minutes, then drain, dry, and chop. Stir the mushrooms and the tomato purée into the casserole.

4 Cover and continue to simmer for another 30 minutes, or until the meat is very tender. Serve while still hot.

GOOD WITH Boiled potatoes, fried bread triangles, and a sprinkling of chopped flat-leaf parsley.

serves 6

prep 30 mins
• cook 2 hrs

flameproof
casserole with
a tight-fitting lid

freeze for up to
3 months

Veal scaloppine

This popular Italian dish uses a classic method to prepare veal.

INGREDIENTS

60g (2oz) plain flour
salt and freshly ground black pepper
4 veal escalopes, about 150g (5½oz) each
60g (2oz) butter
2 tbsp olive oil
60ml (2fl oz) dry white wine
250ml (8fl oz) veal stock or chicken stock
2 tbsp chopped flat-leaf parsley
1 lime, cut into wedges, to serve

METHOD

1 Preheat the oven to its lowest setting. Season the flour with salt and pepper. Put the veal escalopes between 2 sheets of greaseproof paper and pound them with a rolling pin until they are very thin. Coat both sides of the escalopes with the seasoned flour, then shake off the excess, and set aside.

2 Melt two-thirds of the butter with the oil in a large frying pan over a medium heat. Add 2 escalopes and fry for 1–2 minutes on each side, or until golden, pressing down firmly with a spatula to keep the meat as flat as possible. Transfer the escalopes to a plate and keep warm in the oven. Fry the second batch, then remove from the pan and keep warm.

3 Add the wine to the pan, increase the heat, and bubble for 1 minute. Add the stock and the juices from the plate with the escalopes, and continue bubbling until all the liquid is reduced by half. Stir in the parsley, the remaining butter, and season to taste with salt and pepper.

4 Place the escalopes on serving plates and spoon over the pan juices. Serve at once with lime wedges for squeezing over.

GOOD WITH Sautéed spinach and rice or potatoes.

PREPARE AHEAD The escalopes can be pounded in advance, covered, and refrigerated until needed.

serves 4

prep 10 mins
• cook 8 mins

Choucroute garni

This is a simpler, quicker version of a classic dish from Alsac.

INGREDIENTS

3 tbsp goose fat or sunflower oil
250g (9oz) piece smoked gammon, diced
500g (1lb 2oz) pork spare rib, sliced
2 onions, chopped
2 green apples, cored and sliced
1 garlic clove, finely chopped
6 whole black peppercorns, lightly crushed
6 juniper berries, lightly crushed
large sprig of thyme
2 bay leaves
600g jar sauerkraut, thoroughly
  rinsed and drained
300ml (10fl oz) light beer or Riesling wine
500ml (16fl oz) chicken stock
12 small new potatoes
350g (12oz) smoked sausage,
  such as bratwurst or fleischwurst,
  thickly sliced
salt and freshly ground black pepper
parsley, chopped, to garnish

METHOD

1 Heat 2 tbsp goose fat in the casserole and fry the gammon and pork, turning, for 3–4 minutes, or until evenly coloured. Remove the meat and keep warm. Add the onion to the pan and fry for 2–3 minutes.

2 Add the apples, garlic, peppercorns, juniper berries, thyme, and bay leaves. Stir in the sauerkraut, return the gammon and pork to the pan, and add the beer and the stock. Place a piece of greaseproof paper on top of the liquid, cover tightly with a lid, and simmer very gently over a very low heat for 2 hours.

3 Add the potatoes, pushing them down into the sauerkraut, then cover and cook on a low heat for 50–60 minutes, or until tender.

4 Meanwhile, heat the remaining goose fat in a frying pan and fry the sausage quickly until brown, turning once.

5 Spoon the sauerkraut mixture on to a large platter and arrange the smoked sausage on top. Season to taste with salt and pepper, sprinkle with parsley, and serve.

serves 6–8

prep 30 mins
• cook 3 hrs

large
flameproof
casserole

214

Osso bucco

This classic, rich veal stew from Milan is flavoured with garlic and salty anchovies.

INGREDIENTS

3 tbsp plain flour
salt and freshly ground black pepper
4 veal hind shanks, cut into 4cm (1½in) pieces
60g (2oz) butter
4 tbsp olive oil
4 garlic cloves, chopped
½ onion, chopped
4 tbsp tomato purée
about 120ml (4fl oz) beef stock or water
4 tbsp chopped flat-leaf parsley
2 anchovy fillets in oil, drained and chopped
grated zest of 1 lemon

METHOD

1 Season the flour with salt and pepper, then roll the veal in the flour and shake off any excess.

2 Melt the butter with the oil in the casserole. Add the veal, fry for 5 minutes, or until browned on all sides, remove and set aside. Add the garlic and onion to the casserole and fry gently, stirring occasionally, for 5 minutes, or until softened but not browned.

3 Stir in the tomato purée, stock, and salt and pepper to taste and bring to the boil. Reduce the heat to low, cover the casserole and simmer for 1½ hours, or until the veal is tender. Check as it cooks and add more liquid, if necessary. The gravy should be thick but not stiff.

4 To serve, combine the parsley, anchovies, and lemon zest in a bowl. Stir the mixture into the casserole and serve immediately.

GOOD WITH A saffron-flavoured risotto or plain boiled rice.

PREPARE AHEAD The stew can be made up to the end of step 3, left to cool, and chilled for up to 2 days. Reheat gently, then complete step 4.

serves 4

prep 15 mins
• cook 1¾ hrs

ask the butcher
to cut the hind
shanks into
large chunks

large flameproof
casserole

freeze after step
3, once cooled
completely, for
up to 1 month;
thaw completely,
then reheat and
complete step 4

Fabada

This simple Spanish spicy sausage and bacon stew is ideal comfort food, and this time-saving version uses canned beans.

INGREDIENTS

250g (9oz) morcilla (Spanish black pudding)
250g (9oz) chorizo
250g (9oz) thick-cut streaky bacon rashers,
   tocino, or pancetta
1 tbsp olive oil
60ml (2fl oz) red wine
2 x 400g cans white beans, drained
pinch of saffron powder
1 bay leaf
500ml (16fl oz) chicken stock

METHOD

1 Cut the morcilla, chorizo, and bacon into large chunks. Heat the oil in a large saucepan, add the sausages and bacon, and fry, stirring, over a medium-low heat for 2 minutes. Increase the heat, add the wine, and allow it to bubble and reduce for 2–3 minutes.

2 Stir in the beans, the saffron, the bay leaf, and just enough chicken stock to cover. Bring to the boil, reduce the heat, cover, and simmer for 30 minutes. Serve hot.

GOOD WITH Crusty bread.

serves 4

prep 5 mins
• cook 40 mins

Autumn game casserole

Mixed game makes a wonderfully rich-flavoured dish. Look for ready-diced packs of meat, which cut down on preparation time.

INGREDIENTS

2 tbsp olive oil
500g (1lb 2oz) mixed casserole game, such as pheasant, partridge, venison, rabbit, and pigeon, diced
1 onion, sliced
1 carrot, sliced
1 parsnip, sliced
1 fennel bulb, sliced, leaves reserved
2 tbsp plain flour
200ml (7fl oz) dry cider or apple juice
200ml (7fl oz) chicken stock
250g (9oz) chestnut mushrooms, thickly sliced
½ tsp fennel seeds
salt and freshly ground black pepper

METHOD

1 Preheat the oven to 160°C (325°C/Gas 3). Heat the oil in the casserole and fry the diced meats, stirring occasionally, for 3–4 minutes, or until lightly browned. Remove and keep hot.

2 Add the onion, carrot, parsnip, and fennel to the pan and fry, stirring occasionally, for 4–5 minutes, or until lightly coloured. Sprinkle in the flour and gradually stir in the cider and stock. Add the mushrooms and fennel seeds, then return the meat to the pan.

3 Season well and bring to the boil. Cover tightly with a lid and place in the oven for 1 hour 20 minutes, or until the meat and vegetables are tender.

4 Sprinkle the casserole with the reserved fennel leaves or chopped parsley, and serve hot.

PREPARE AHEAD The casserole can be prepared up to 2 days in advance, then cooled and stored in the refrigerator. Reheat and serve.

serves 4

prep 20 mins
• cook 1 hr
30 mins

flameproof
casserole

freeze for up to
3 months

ACKNOWLEDGMENTS

DORLING KINDERSLEY WOULD LIKE TO THANK THE FOLLOWING:

Photographers
Steve Baxter, Martin Brigdale, Tony Cambio, Nigel Gibson, Francesco Guillamet, Adrian Heapy, Jeff Kauck, David Munns, David Murray, Ian O'Leary, Roddy Paine, William Reavell, Gavin Sawyer, William Shaw, Carole Tuff, Kieran Watson, Stuart West, Jon Whitaker

Prop Stylist
Sue Rowlands

Food Stylist
Jennifer White

Picture Research
Emma Shepherd

Index
Susan Bosanko

Useful information

Refrigerator and freezer storage guidelines

FOOD	REFRIGERATOR	FREEZER
Raw poultry, fish, and meat (small pieces)	2–3 days	3–6 months
Raw minced beef and poultry	1–2 days	3 months
Cooked whole roasts or whole poultry	2–3 days	9 months
Cooked poultry pieces	1–2 days	1 month (6 months in stock or gravy)
Soups and stews	2–3 days	1–3 months
Casseroles	2–3 days	2–4 weeks

Oven temperature equivalents

CELSIUS	FAHRENHEIT	GAS	DESCRIPTION
110°C	225°F	¼	Cool
130°C	250°F	½	Cool
140°C	275°F	1	Very low
150°C	300°F	2	Very low
160°C	325°F	3	Low
180°C	350°F	4	Moderate
190°C	375°F	5	Moderately hot
200°C	400°F	6	Hot
220°C	425°F	7	Hot
230°C	450°F	8	Very hot
240°C	475°F	9	Very hot